WHAT'S COOKING

barbecue

Salads for Summer

Jacqueline Bellefontaine

WHITECAP BOOKS

This edition published in 1998 by
WHITECAP BOOKS
351 Lynn Avenue
North Vancouver, B.C., V7J 2C4

ISBN: 1-55110-746-5

Printed in Italy

Produced by Haldane Mason, London

Acknowledgments
Art Director: Ron Samuels
Editorial Director: Sydney Francis
Editorial Consultant: Christopher Fagg
Managing Editor: Jo-Anne Cox
Editor: Lydia Darbyshire
Design: Digital Artworks Partnership Ltd
Photography: St John Asprey
Home Economist: Jacqueline Bellefontaine

Note
Cup measurements in this book are for standard American cups.
Unless otherwise stated, milk is assumed to be homogenized, eggs are medium,
and pepper is freshly ground black pepper.

The barbecues used for the photography in this book were kindly supplied by:
Weber, Yardley Road, Knowsley Industrial Park North, Kirkby, Liverpool, UK
and Castle Catering Supplies, 4 King James Court, London, UK.

Contents

Introduction   4

Fish & Seafood   6

Poultry   48

Meat   94

Vegetables & Salads   172

Desserts   234

Index   256

Introduction

What is it that makes a meal cooked outdoors over burning coals so appetizing? Perhaps it's the fresh air, or the tantalizing aroma, or the sound of food sizzling on the cooking rack. Whatever it is, there is no doubt that barbecues are becoming more and more popular. This is hardly surprising when you see just how many wonderful dishes can be cooked over charcoal. This book alone contains 120 recipes, leaving you with no shortage of inspiration.

Gone are the days when sausages and hamburgers were the staple of every barbecue party, although traditionalists will find recipes here for making fabulous burgers and for tangy sauces to serve with the sausages. But why not try fish, which cooks to perfection on the barbecue and is healthy too? There are also dozens of tasty marinades and bastes for meat lovers, as well as vegetarian dishes, salads, and side dishes. You can even cook a dessert on the barbecue.

WHICH BARBECUE?

You do not need a large, sophisticated barbecue to produce mouthwatering food, although once you have tried some of these recipes you might want to invest in something larger.

Essentially barbecues are an open fire with a rack set over the hot coals, on which the food is cooked. You can improvise a makeshift barbecue with nothing more complicated than a few house bricks and an old oven rack. **Chicken wire** and **baking racks** can also be used to cook on. Purpose-made barbecues are, however, available in all shapes and sizes, from small disposable trays to large wagon, gas-powered models.

As the names suggest, **portable** and **semiportable barbecues** tend to be small. Some types have a stand or folding legs; others have fixed legs. If you have a small model and are cooking for large numbers, cook the food in rotation so that guests can begin on the first course while the second batch is cooking.

Most **brazier barbecues,** which stand on long legs and have a windshield, are light and portable. On some models the height of the rack can be varied, and some types incorporate electrically-powered rotisseries.

Covered barbecues are essential if you want to cook whole joints of meat. The lid completely covers the barbecue, increasing the temperature at which food cooks and acting, in effect, like an oven. The temperature is controlled by air vents. When used without the cover, these barbecues are treated like a traditional barbecue.

Wagon barbecues are larger, more sophisticated and quite expensive. They have wheels and often incorporate a tabletop.

Electric or **gas barbecues** heat volcanic lava coals. The flavor is still good, because the flavor of barbecued food comes from the aromas of fat and juices burning on the coals, rather than the fuel itself.

EQUIPMENT

Apart from the barbecue itself, you do not need any special equipment, but do protect yourself with a pair of **potholders**. **Long-handled tools** can be useful, as well as being safer, and more convenient to use. They are not expensive, and if you cook on a barbecue regularly, it is a good idea to invest in a set. **Racks** for burgers, sausages, and fish are useful, but not essential.

You will need a set of **skewers** if you want to cook kabobs. *Metal skewers* should be flat to stop the food slipping round as it cooks. Remember that metal skewers get very hot, so wear potholders or use *tongs* to turn them. *Wooden skewers* are much cheaper than metal skewers, but are not always very long lasting. Always soak wooden skewers in cold water for at least 30 minutes before use to help prevent them from burning on the barbecue, and then cover the exposed ends with pieces of kitchen foil.

A **water spray** is useful for cooling down coals or dampening down flare-ups.

LIGHTING THE BARBECUE

Charcoal is the most popular fuel although you can use some wood. Charcoal is available as *lump wood*, which is irregular in shape and size, but easy to light, or as *briquettes*, which burn for longer and with a more uniform heat, but are harder to light.

Light the barbecue at least an hour before you want to start cooking. Stack the coals in the pan and use specially designed solid or liquid barbecue lighter fuels to help set the charcoal alight. Do not use household fire lighters because these will taint the food. Never use kerosene or petrol to light a barbecue—both of these are very dangerous if used incorrectly in this way and would not only taint the food, but could also result in serious injury.

The barbecue is ready to use when the flames have died down and the coals are covered with a thin layer of white ash. When the coals are sufficiently hot, spread them out into a uniform layer.

PREPARING TO COOK

Before you begin to cook, oil the rack so that the food does not stick to it. Do this away from the barbecue or the oil will flare up as it drips onto the coals. For most dishes, position the rack about 3 inches above the coals. Raise the rack if you want to slow down the cooking. If you cannot adjust the height of the rack, slow down the cooking by spreading out the coals or moving the food to the edges of the rack, where the heat will be less intense.

If your barbecue has air vents, use them to control the temperature—open the vents for more heat and close them when you need to reduce the temperature.

It is very difficult to give exact times for cooking on a barbecue, so use the times given in the recipes in this book as guidelines only. Always test the food, particularly pork and chicken, to make sure that it is cooked thoroughly before serving.

Fish & Seafood

Fish tastes wonderful when it is cooked on the barbecue. This chapter is full of ideas, ranging from simple charbroiled whole fish to spicy marinated packets and kabobs. Oily fish is especially suitable for the barbecue because the flesh does not dry out over the direct heat. White fish will benefit from the addition of a baste or marinade if it is cooked directly over the coals, but smaller fish can be cooked whole, because the skin keeps in all the wonderful juices and acts as a natural protective coating. Barbecue fish steaks with a marinade or baste directly on the rack.

Choose a fish with a firm flesh or it may break up and drop on to the coals when you turn it. Alternatively, invest in a hinged rack, which will make turning infinitely easier. A firm fish, such as monkfish, is essential for skewers, and wrap more delicate fish in kitchen foil, so that it cooks in its own juice.

Seafood is quick to cook and does not need to be left in a marinade for long, making it ideal for impromptu barbecues. Shrimp skewers, for example, can be made and cooked in minutes.

Indonesian-style Spicy Cod

A delicious aromatic coating makes this dish rather special.
Serve it with a crisp salad and crusty bread.

Serves 4

INGREDIENTS

4 cod steaks
1 stalk lemon grass
1 small red onion, chopped
3 cloves garlic, chopped
2 fresh red chilies, seeded
  and chopped

1 tsp grated fresh ginger root
$1/4$ tsp turmeric
2 tbsp butter, cut into small cubes
8 tbsp canned coconut milk
2 tbsp lemon juice

salt and pepper
red chilies, to garnish (optional)

1 Rinse the cod steaks and pat them dry on absorbent paper towels.

2 Remove and discard the outer leaves from the lemon grass stalk and thinly slice the inner section.

3 Place the lemon grass, onion, garlic, chili, ginger, and turmeric in a food processor and blend until the ingredients are finely chopped. Season with salt and pepper to taste.

4 With the processor running, add the butter, coconut milk, and lemon juice and process until well blended.

5 Place the fish in a shallow, nonmetallic dish. Pour the coconut mixture on top and turn the fish until well coated.

6 If you have one, place the fish steaks in a hinged basket, which will make them easier to turn. Broil over hot coals for 15 minutes or until the fish is

cooked through, turning once. Serve garnished with red chilies, if desired.

COOK'S TIP

If you prefer a milder flavor, omit the chilies altogether. For a hotter flavor do not remove the seeds from the chilies.

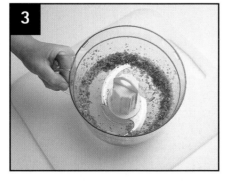

Blackened Fish

The word "blackened" refers to the spicy marinade that is used to coat the fish and that chars slightly as it cooks. Choose a fish with a firm texture, such as hake or halibut.

Serves 4

INGREDIENTS

4 white fish steaks
1 tbsp paprika
1 tsp dried thyme
1 tsp cayenne pepper

1 tsp freshly ground black pepper
$1/2$ tsp freshly ground white pepper
$1/2$ tsp salt
$1/4$ tsp ground allspice

4 tbsp unsalted butter
3 tbsp sunflower oil

1 Rinse the fish steaks and pat them dry with absorbent paper towels.

2 Mix together the paprika, thyme, cayenne pepper, black and white peppers, salt, and allspice in a shallow dish.

3 Place the butter and oil in a small saucepan and heat, stirring occasionally, until the butter melts.

4 Brush the butter mixture liberally all over the fish steaks, on both sides.

5 Dip the fish into the spicy mix until well coated on both sides.

6 Broil the fish over hot coals for about 10 minutes on each side, turning it over once. Continue to baste the fish with the remaining butter mixture during the cooking time.

COOK'S TIP

Basting the fish with the butter mixture will ensure that the fish remains moist during cooking.

VARIATION

A whole fish—red mullet, for example—rather than steaks is also delicious cooked this way. The spicy seasoning can also be used to coat chicken portions, if you prefer.

Monkfish Skewers with Zucchini & Lemon

A simple basting sauce is brushed over these tasty kabobs, which make a perfect light meal on their own.

Serves 4

INGREDIENTS

1 pound monkfish tail
2 zucchini
1 lemon
12 cherry tomatoes
8 bay leaves

SAUCE:
4 tbsp olive oil
2 tbsp lemon juice
1 tsp chopped, fresh thyme
1/2 tsp lemon pepper
salt

TO SERVE:
salad greens
fresh, crusty bread

1 Cut the monkfish into 2-inch chunks. Cut the zucchini into thick slices and the lemon into wedges.

2 Thread the monkfish chunks, zucchini slices, lemon wedges, tomatoes, and bay leaves onto 4 skewers.

3 To make the basting sauce, combine the oil, lemon juice, thyme, lemon pepper, and salt to taste in a small bowl.

4 Brush the basting sauce liberally all over the fish, lemon, tomatoes, and bay leaves on the skewers.

5 Cook the skewers on the barbecue for about 15 minutes, basting frequently with the sauce, until the fish is cooked through.

6 Serve the kabobs with salad greens and warm, fresh crusty bread.

VARIATION

Use flounder fillets instead of the monkfish, if you prefer. Allow two fillets per person, and skin and cut each fillet lengthwise into two. Roll up each piece and thread them onto the skewers.

Monkfish Skewers with Coconut & Cilantro

This is a tasty kabob with a mild marinade. Allow the skewers to marinate for at least an hour before cooking.

Serves 4

INGREDIENTS

1 pound monkfish tails
8 ounces raw peeled shrimp
shredded coconut, toasted, to
   garnish (optional)

MARINADE:
1 tsp sunflower oil
$1/2$ small onion, finely grated
1 tsp fresh ginger root, grated

$2/3$ cup canned coconut milk
2 tbsp chopped, fresh cilantro

1   To make the marinade, heat the oil in a wok or saucepan and sauté the onion and ginger for 5 minutes, until just softened but not browned.

2   Add the coconut milk to the pan and bring to a boil. Boil rapidly for about 5 minutes, or until reduced to the consistency of light cream.

3   Remove the pan from the heat and allow to cool completely. Once cooled, stir in the cilantro and pour into a shallow dish.

4   Cut the fish into bite-size chunks and stir gently into the coconut mixture, together with the shrimp. Chill in the refrigerator for 1–4 hours.

5   Thread the fish and shrimp onto skewers and discard any remaining marinade. Broil the skewers over hot coals for 10–15 minutes, turning frequently. Garnish with toasted coconut, if desired.

VARIATION

Look for uncooked shrimp in the freezer section in large supermarkets. If you cannot obtain them, you can use cooked shrimp, but remember they only need heating through.

Charred Tuna Steaks

Tuna has a firm flesh, which is ideal for barbecuing, but it can be a little dry unless it is marinated first.

Serves 4

INGREDIENTS

4 tuna steaks
3 tbsp soy sauce
1 tbsp Worcestershire sauce
1 tsp wholegrain mustard

1 tsp superfine sugar
1 tbsp sunflower oil
salad greens, to serve

TO GARNISH:
parsley
lemon wedges

1 Place the tuna steaks in a shallow dish.

2 Mix together the soy sauce, Worcestershire sauce, mustard, sugar, and oil in a small bowl. Pour the marinade over the tuna steaks.

3 Gently turn the tuna steaks, using your fingers or a fork, so that they are well coated with the marinade.

4 Cover and place the tuna steaks in the refrigerator and chill for between 30 minutes and 2 hours.

5 Broil the marinated fish over hot coals for 10–15 minutes, turning once. Baste frequently with any of the marinade that is left in the dish.

6 Garnish with parsley and lemon wedges, and serve with a fresh salad greens.

COOK'S TIP

If a marinade contains soy sauce, the marinating time should be limited, usually to 2 hours. If allowed to marinate for too long, the fish will dry out and become tough.

COOK'S TIP

Tuna has a dark red flesh, which turns paler on cooking. Tuna has a good meaty texture, but if you are unable to obtain it, use swordfish steaks instead.

Charbroiled Bream

*Bream have quite tough scales, which need to be removed before cooking.
Ask your supplier to do this for you. A single sea bream is the ideal size for one person.*

Serves 2

INGREDIENTS

2 small sea bream, scaled, gutted,
   trimmed, and cleaned
2 slices lemon
2 bay leaves
salt and pepper

BASTE:
4 tbsp olive oil
2 tbsp lemon juice
1/2 tsp chopped, fresh oregano
1/2 tsp chopped, fresh thyme

TO GARNISH:
fresh bay leaves
fresh thyme sprig
lemon wedges

1 Using a sharp knife, cut 2–3 deep slashes into the bodies of both fish in order to help them fully absorb the flavor of the basting sauce.

2 Place a slice of lemon and a bay leaf inside the cavity of each fish. Season inside the cavity with salt and pepper.

3 In a small bowl, mix together the ingredients for the baste using a fork. Alternatively, place the basting ingredients in a small screw-top jar and shake well to combine thoroughly.

4 Brush some of the baste liberally over the fish and place them on a rack over hot coals. Broil over hot coals for 20–30 minutes, turning and basting frequently.

5 Transfer the fish to a serving plate, garnish with fresh bay leaves, thyme, and lemon wedges, and serve.

VARIATION

If you prefer, use brill or a fish like gurnard instead of the sea bream.

COOK'S TIP

The flavor of the dish will be enhanced if you use good fresh ingredients in the sauce. Dried herbs can be used, but remember that the flavor is much more intense, so only use half the quantity of the fresh herbs listed above.

Salmon Yakitori

The Japanese sauce used here combines well with salmon, although it is usually served with chicken.

Serves 4

INGREDIENTS

12 ounces chunky salmon fillet
8 baby leeks

YAKITORI SAUCE:
5 tbsp light soy sauce
5 tbsp fish stock
2 tbsp superfine sugar
5 tbsp dry white wine

3 tbsp sweet sherry
1 clove garlic, crushed

1 Skin the salmon and cut the flesh into 2-inch chunks. Trim the leeks and cut them into 2-inch lengths.

2 Thread the salmon and leeks alternately onto 8 presoaked wooden skewers. Chill in the refrigerator until required.

3 To make the sauce, place all of the ingredients in a small pan and heat gently, stirring, until the sugar dissolves. Bring to a boil, then reduce the heat, and simmer for 2 minutes. Strain the sauce and leave to cool.

4 Pour about one-third of the sauce into a small dish and then set aside to serve with the kabobs.

5 Brush plenty of the remaining sauce over the skewers and cook directly on the rack or, if preferred, place a sheet of greased foil on the rack and cook the salmon on that. Broil the skewers over hot coals for about 10 minutes, turning once. Baste the skewers frequently during cooking with the remaining sauce to prevent the fish and vegetables from drying out.

6 Serve the kabobs with the dish of reserved sauce for dipping.

COOK'S TIP

Soak the wooden skewers in cold water for at least 30 minutes to prevent them from burning during cooking. You can make the kabobs and sauce several hours ahead of time. Keep in the refrigerator until required.

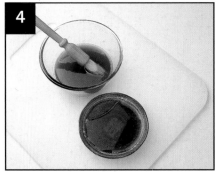

Salmon Brochettes

These tasty kabobs have a lovely summery flavor.
Serve on a bread croûte with fresh tomato sauce.

Serves 4

INGREDIENTS

1 pound salmon, skinned and cut
   into large chunks
1 tbsp cornstarch
$1/2$ tsp salt
$1/2$ tsp pepper
1 small egg white, beaten
1 red bell pepper, seeded and cut
   into chunks

1 green bell pepper, seeded and cut
   into chunks
4 tbsp olive oil
Italian bread, to serve

TOMATO SAUCE:
4 tomatoes, seeded and quartered
$1/4$ cucumber, peeled, seeded,
   and chopped
8 basil leaves
6 tbsp olive oil
2 tbsp lemon juice
salt and pepper

1 Place the salmon in a shallow dish and sprinkle the cornstarch and salt and pepper on top. Add the beaten egg white and toss well to coat. Chill for 15 minutes.

2 Thread the pieces of salmon onto 4 skewers, alternating the fish pieces with the chunks of red and green bell peppers. Set the skewers aside while you make the tomato sauce.

3 To make the sauce, place all of the ingredients in a food processor and chop coarsely. Alternatively, chop the tomatoes, cucumber, and basil leaves by hand and mix with the oil, lemon juice, and seasoning. Let chill.

4 Broil the salmon brochettes over hot coals for 10 minutes, brushing frequently with olive oil to prevent them from drying during cooking.

5 Slice the Italian bread at an angle to produce 4 long slices. Lightly toast on the barbecue.

6 Spread the sauce over each slice of bread and top with a salmon brochette.

VARIATION

Serve the salmon brochettes on
toasted French baguettes if preferred.

Japanese-style Charbroiled Flounder

The marinade for this dish has a distinctly Japanese flavor, which goes well with any white fish.

Serves 4

INGREDIENTS

4 small flounders	1 tbsp lemon juice	TO GARNISH:
6 tbsp soy sauce	2 tbsp light muscovado sugar	1 small carrot
2 tbsp sake or dry white wine	1 tsp fresh ginger root, grated	4 scallions
2 tbsp sesame oil	1 clove garlic, crushed	

1 Rinse the fish and pat them dry on absorbent paper towels. Cut a few slashes into both sides of each fish.

2 Mix together the soy sauce, sake or wine, oil, lemon juice, sugar, ginger, and garlic in a large, shallow dish.

3 Place the fish in the marinade and turn them over so that they are well coated on both sides. Let stand in the refrigerator for 1–6 hours.

4 Meanwhile, prepare the garnish. Using a sharp knife, cut the carrot into even-size thin sticks and clean and shred the scallions.

5 Broil the fish over hot coals for about 10 minutes, turning them once.

6 Scatter the chopped scallions and sliced carrot over the fish and then transfer the fish to a warm serving dish. Serve immediately.

VARIATION

Use sole instead of the flounders, and scatter over some toasted sesame seeds instead of the carrot and scallions, if you prefer.

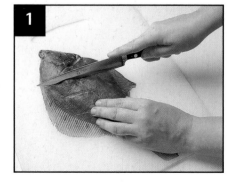

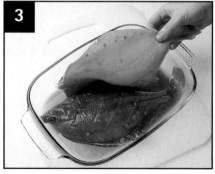

Smoky Fish Skewers

The combination of fresh and smoked fish gives these kabobs a special flavor. Choose thick fish fillets to get good size pieces.

Serves 4

INGREDIENTS

12 ounces smoked cod fillet
12 ounces cod fillet
8 large raw shrimp
8 bay leaves
fresh dill, to garnish (optional)

MARINADE:
4 tbsp sunflower oil
2 tbsp lemon or lime juice
rind of ¹/₂ lemon or lime, grated

¹/₄ tsp dried dill
salt and pepper

1 Skin both types of cod and cut the flesh into bite-size pieces. Peel the shrimp, leaving just the tail.

2 To make the marinade, combine the sunflower oil, lemon or lime juice, grated lemon or lime rind, dried dill, and salt and pepper to taste in a shallow, nonmetallic dish.

3 Place the prepared fish in the marinade and stir together until the fish is well coated on all sides. Marinate in the refrigerator for 1–4 hours.

4 Thread the fish onto 4 skewers, alternating the 2 types of cod with the shrimp and bay leaves.

5 Cover the rack with lightly buttered foil and place the fish skewers on top of the foil.

6 Broil the fish skewers over hot coals for 5–10 minutes, basting with any remaining marinade, turning once.

7 Garnish with fresh dill, if using, and serve.

COOK'S TIP

Cod fillet is inclined to flake, so choose the thicker end which is easier to cut into chunky pieces. Line the rack with foil rather than cooking the fish directly on the rack so that, even if the fish does break away from the skewer, it is not wasted.

Apricot Charbroiled Mackerel

*The sharpness of the apricot glaze complements the oiliness
of the fish and has a delicious hint of ginger.*

Serves 4

INGREDIENTS

4 mackerel	3 tbsp Worcestershire sauce	dash Tabasco sauce
14 ounce can apricots in natural juice	3 tbsp soy sauce	1 clove garlic, crushed (optional)
3 tbsp dark muscovado sugar	2 tbsp tomato paste	salt and pepper
	1 tsp ground ginger	

1 Clean and gut the mackerel, removing the heads if preferred. Place the fish in a shallow dish.

2 Drain the apricots, reserving the juice. Roughly chop half of the apricots and set aside.

3 Place the remaining apricots in a food processor with the sugar, Worcestershire sauce, soy sauce, tomato paste, ginger, Tabasco sauce, and garlic (if using) and process until smooth. Alternatively, chop the apricots and mix with the other ingredients.

4 Pour the sauce over the fish, turning them so that they are well coated on both sides. Chill in the refrigerator until they are required.

5 Transfer the mackerel to the barbecue either directly on the rack or on a piece of greased kitchen foil. Broil the mackerel over hot coals for 5–7 minutes, turning once.

6 Spoon any remaining marinade into a saucepan. Add the reserved chopped apricots and about half of the reserved apricot juice, and bring to a boil. Reduce the heat and simmer for 2 minutes.

7 Transfer the mackerel to a serving plate and serve with the apricot sauce.

COOK'S TIP

Use a hinged rack if you have one, as it will make it much easier to turn the fish while it is cooking.

Mackerel with Lime & Cilantro

The secret of this dish lies in the simple, fresh flavors which perfectly complement the fish.

Serves 4

INGREDIENTS

4 small mackerel
¼ tsp ground coriander
¼ tsp ground cumin
4 sprigs fresh cilantro

3 tbsp chopped, fresh cilantro
1 red chili, seeded and chopped
grated rind and juice of 1 lime

2 tbsp sunflower oil
salt and pepper
1 lime, sliced, to garnish
chili flowers, to garnish (optional)
salad greens, to serve

1 To make the chili flowers (if using), cut the tip of a small chili lengthwise into thin strips, leaving the chili intact at the stem end. Remove the seeds and place in iced water until curled.

2 Clean and gut the mackerel, removing the heads if preferred. Transfer the mackerel to a chopping board.

3 Sprinkle the fish with the ground spices and salt and pepper to taste. Place a sprig of fresh cilantro inside the cavity of each fish.

4 Mix together the chopped cilantro, chili, lime rind and juice, and the oil in a small bowl. Brush the mixture liberally over the fish.

5 Place the fish in a hinged rack if you have one. Broil the fish over hot coals for 3–4 minutes on each side, turning once. Brush frequently with the remaining basting mixture.

6 Garnish with lime slices and chili flowers, if using, and serve with salad greens.

VARIATION

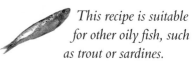

This recipe is suitable for other oily fish, such as trout or sardines.

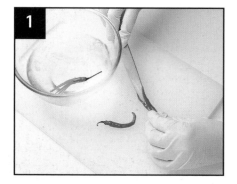

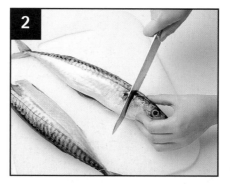

Mediterranean-style Sardines

These tasty sardines will bring back memories of Mediterranean vacations.
Serve them with crusty brown bread as a perfect starter.

Serves 4

INGREDIENTS

8–12 fresh sardines
8–12 sprigs of fresh thyme
3 tbsp lemon juice

4 tbsp olive oil
salt and pepper

TO GARNISH:
lemon wedges
tomato slices
fresh herbs

1 Clean and gut the fish if this has not already been done by the fish store or supermarket.

2 Remove the scales from the sardines by rubbing the back of a knife from head to tail along the body. Wash and pat the sardines dry on absorbent paper towels.

3 Tuck a sprig of fresh thyme into the body of each sardine.

4 Transfer the sardines to a large, nonmetallic dish and season with salt and pepper to taste.

5 Beat together the lemon juice and oil in a bowl and pour the mixture over the sardines. Let the sardines marinate in the refrigerator for about 30 minutes.

6 Remove the sardines from the marinade and place them in a hinged basket, if you have one, or on a rack. Broil the sardines over hot coals for 3–4 minutes on each side, basting them frequently with any of the remaining marinade.

7 Serve the sardines garnished with lemon wedges, tomato slices, and fresh herbs.

COOK'S TIP

Look out for small sardines or sprats. Prepare them as above and use the same marinade. Place a piece of greased foil on the rack and cook over hot coals for 2–3 minutes on each side.

VARIATION

For a slightly different flavor and texture, toss the sardines in dried breadcrumbs and then baste them with a little olive oil for a crispy coating.

Nutty Stuffed Trout

Stuff the trout just before cooking. If you prefer, the fish can be cooked in foil packets on the barbecue.

Serves 4

INGREDIENTS

4 medium trout, cleaned
2 tbsp sunflower oil
1 small onion, finely chopped
1/2 cup toasted mixed
   nuts, chopped

rind of 1 orange, grated
2 tbsp orange juice
1 3/4 cups fresh whole-
   wheat breadcrumbs
1 medium egg, beaten

oil for brushing
salt and pepper
orange slices, to garnish
orange and watercress salad, to serve

1 Season the trout inside and out with salt and pepper.

2 To make the stuffing, heat the oil in a small saucepan and sauté the onion until soft. Remove the pan from the heat and stir in the chopped nuts, grated orange rind, orange juice, and the whole-wheat breadcrumbs. Add just enough beaten egg to bind the mixture together.

3 Divide the stuffing into 4 equal portions and spoon into the body of each fish.

4 Brush the fish liberally with oil and broil over medium hot coals for 10 minutes on each side, turning once. When the fish is cooked, the flesh will be white and firm and the skin will be beginning to crisp.

5 Transfer the fish to individual serving plates and garnish with orange slices.

6 Serve the fish with an orange and watercress salad and an orange and mustard dressing (see Cook's Tip).

COOK'S TIP

Serve the stuffed trout with an orange and watercress salad. For the dressing, mix together 2 tbsp orange juice, 1 tbsp white wine vinegar, 3 tbsp olive oil, 1/2 tsp wholegrain mustard, and salt and pepper to taste. Pour the dressing over the orange and watercress salad just before serving.

Barbecued Herrings with Lemon

*Cook these fish in foil packets for a wonderfully
moist texture. They make a perfect starter.*

Serves 4

INGREDIENTS

4 herrings, cleaned
4 bay leaves
salt

1 lemon, sliced
4 tbsp unsalted butter
2 tbsp chopped, fresh parsley

$^1/_2$ tsp lemon pepper
fresh crusty bread, to serve

1 Season the prepared herrings inside and out with freshly ground salt to taste.

2 Place a bay leaf inside the cavity of each fish.

3 Place 4 squares of foil on the counter and divide the lemon slices evenly among them. Place one fish on top of the lemon slices.

4 Beat the butter until softened, then mix in the parsley and lemon pepper. Dot the flavored butter liberally all over the fish.

5 Wrap the fish tightly in the foil and cook over medium hot coals for about 15–20 minutes, or until the fish is cooked through—the flesh should be white in color and firm to the touch (unwrap the foil to check, then wrap up the fish again).

6 Transfer the wrapped fish packets to individual, warm serving plates.

7 Unwrap the foil parcels just before serving and serve the fish with fresh, crusty bread to mop up the deliciously flavored cooking juices.

VARIATION

For a main course use trout instead of herring. Cook for 20–30 minutes, until the flesh is firm to the touch and opaque.

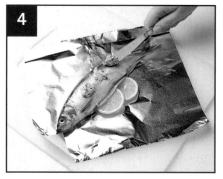

Sardines with Olives & Tomatoes

Tomatoes flavored with basil and olives make sardines into a tasty meal.

Serves 4

INGREDIENTS

12 fresh sardines, gutted and cleaned
fresh basil leaves
4 plum tomatoes
8 pitted black olives

1 tbsp butter
1 tbsp olive oil
2 tbsp lemon juice
salt and pepper

TO GARNISH:
plum tomatoes, sliced
pitted olives, sliced
1 fresh basil sprig

1 Season the sardines inside and out with salt and pepper to taste. Insert 1–2 basil leaves inside the cavity of each fish. Using a sharp knife, make a few slashes in the body of each fish.

2 Cut the tomatoes and olives into slices and transfer to a large bowl. Tear 4 basil leaves into small pieces and toss together with the tomatoes and olives.

3 Divide the tomato and olive mixture among 4 large sheets of foil, and place 3 sardines on top of each portion.

4 Melt the butter and oil together in a small pan. Stir in the lemon juice and pour the mixture over the fish.

5 Carefully wrap up the fish in the foil. Cook the fish over medium hot coals for 15–20 minutes until the fish is firm and cooked through.

6 Transfer the fish to individual serving plates and remove the foil. Garnish the fish with slices of tomato and olive, and with a fresh sprig of basil. Serve at once.

COOK'S TIP

Slashing the body of the fish helps the flesh to absorb the flavors. It is particularly important if you do not have time to allow the fish to marinate before cooking.

VARIATION

You can barbecue trout or mackerel in exactly the same way as the sardines, but remember to increase the cooking time to 20–30 minutes.

Bacon & Scallop Skewers

Wrapping bacon around the scallops helps to protect the delicate flesh from the intense heat and allows them to cook without becoming tough. The bacon also imparts a subtle smoky flavor to the scallops.

Makes 4

INGREDIENTS

grated rind and juice of $^1/_2$ lemon
4 tbsp sunflower oil
$^1/_2$ tsp dried dill

12 scallops
1 red bell pepper
1 green bell pepper

1 yellow bell pepper
6 slices bacon

1 Mix together the lemon rind and juice, sunflower oil, and dried dill in a nonmetallic dish. Add the scallops and mix thoroughly to coat in the marinade. Marinate for 1–2 hours in the refrigerator.

2 Cut the red, green, and yellow bell peppers in half and seed them. Cut the bell pepper halves into 1-inch pieces and then set aside in a small bowl until required.

3 Carefully stretch the bacon slices with the back of a knife blade, then cut each bacon slice in half.

4 Remove the scallops from the marinade, reserving any excess marinade. Wrap a piece of bacon around each scallop.

5 Thread the bacon-wrapped scallops onto skewers, alternating with the bell pepper pieces.

6 Broil the bacon and scallop skewers over hot coals for about 5 minutes, basting frequently with the lemon and oil marinade.

7 Transfer the bacon and scallop skewers to serving plates and serve at once.

VARIATION

Peel 4–8 raw shrimp and add them to the marinade with the scallops. Thread them onto the skewers alternately with the scallops and bell peppers.

COOK'S TIP

Hold the hot skewers with potholders when you are turning them on the barbecue.

Herrings with Orange Tarragon Stuffing

*The fish are filled with an orange-flavored stuffing and are wrapped
in kitchen foil before being baked on the barbecue.*

Serves 4

INGREDIENTS

1 orange	4 herrings, cleaned and gutted	TO GARNISH:
4 scallions	salt and pepper	2 oranges
1 cup fresh whole-	salad greens, to serve	1 tbsp light brown sugar
wheat breadcrumbs		1 tbsp olive oil
1 tbsp fresh tarragon, chopped		sprigs of fresh tarragon

1 To make the stuffing, grate the rind from half of the orange, using a zester.

2 Peel and chop all of the orange flesh on a plate in order to catch all of the juice.

3 Mix together the orange flesh, juice, rind, scallions, breadcrumbs, and tarragon in a bowl. Season with salt and pepper to taste.

4 Divide the stuffing into 4 equal portions and use it to fill the body cavities of the fish.

5 Place each fish onto a square of lightly greased kitchen foil and wrap the foil around the fish so that it is completely enclosed. Cook over hot coals for 20–30 minutes, until the fish are cooked through—the flesh should be white and firm to the touch.

6 Meanwhile, make the garnish. Peel and thickly slice the 2 oranges and sprinkle with the sugar. Just before the fish is cooked, drizzle a little oil over the orange slices and place them on the barbecue for about 5 minutes to heat through.

7 Transfer the fish to serving plates and garnish with the barbecued orange slices and sprigs of fresh tarragon. Serve with salad greens.

VARIATION

Use any oily fish for this dish—trout and mackerel are ideal. In addition, try lemons instead of oranges for a different citrusy flavor.

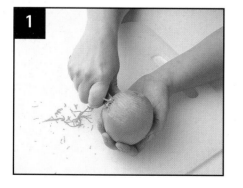

Caribbean Shrimp

This is an ideal recipe for cooks who have difficulty in finding raw shrimp.

Serves 4

INGREDIENTS

16 cooked tiger shrimp
1 small pineapple
flaked coconut, to garnish (optional)

MARINADE:
2/3 cup pineapple juice
2 tbsp white wine vinegar

2 tbsp dark muscovado sugar
2 tbsp shredded coconut

1 If they are unpeeled, peel the shrimp, leaving the tails attached if preferred.

2 Peel the pineapple and cut it in half lengthwise. Cut one pineapple half into wedges, then into chunks.

3 To make the marinade, mix together half of the pineapple juice and the vinegar, sugar, and coconut in a shallow, nonmetallic dish. Add the peeled shrimp and pineapple chunks and toss until well coated. Marinate the shrimp and pineapple for at least 30 minutes in the refrigerator.

4 Remove the pineapple and shrimp from the marinade and thread them onto skewers. Reserve the marinade.

5 Strain the marinade and place in a food processor. Roughly chop the remaining pineapple and add to the processor with the remaining pineapple juice. Process the pineapple for a few seconds to produce a thick sauce.

6 Pour the sauce into a small saucepan. Bring to a boil, then simmer for about 5 minutes. This can be done by the side of the barbecue if preferred.

7 Transfer the kabobs to the barbecue and brush with some of the sauce. Broil for about 5 minutes until the kabobs are piping hot. Turn the kabobs, brushing occasionally with the sauce. Serve with extra sauce, sprinkled with flaked coconut (if using), on the side.

COOK'S TIP

Barbecue these kabobs just long enough to heat through. If they are cooked for too long, the shrimp will toughen.

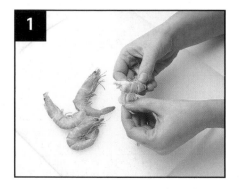

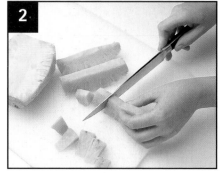

Herb & Garlic Shrimp

*Look for raw shrimp in the freezer section
of large supermarkets or Chinese food stores.*

Serves 4

INGREDIENTS

12 ounces raw shrimp, peeled
2 tbsp chopped, fresh parsley

4 tbsp lemon juice
2 tbsp olive oil
5 tbsp butter

2 cloves garlic, chopped
salt and pepper

1 Place the prepared shrimp in a shallow, nonmetallic dish with the parsley, lemon juice, and salt and pepper to taste. Stir gently to mix. Marinate the shrimp in the herb mixture for at least 30 minutes in the refrigerator.

2 Heat the oil and butter in a small pan, together with the garlic, until the butter melts. Stir to mix thoroughly.

3 Remove the shrimp from the marinade with a slotted spoon and add them to the pan containing the garlic butter. Stir the shrimp into the garlic butter until well coated all over, then thread the shrimp onto several skewers.

4 Broil the kabobs over hot coals for 5–10 minutes, turning the skewers occasionally, until the shrimp turn pink and are cooked through. Generously brush the shrimp with the remaining garlic butter during the cooking time.

5 Transfer the herb and garlic shrimp kabobs to serving plates. Drizzle over any of the remaining garlic butter and serve at once.

VARIATION

If raw shrimp are unavailable, use cooked shrimp, but reduce the cooking time. Small cooked shrimp can also be cooked in a foil packet instead of on the skewers. Marinate and toss the cooked shrimp in the garlic butter, wrap in foil, and cook for about 5 minutes, shaking the packets once or twice.

Poultry

Poultry is a versatile food that can be cooked in a number of ways on the barbecue. Try it with herbs and garlic, tangy tomato glazes, or spicy Asian flavors. It also goes well with sweet glazes and fruit.

Chicken is ideal for the barbecue because the skin helps to keep the flesh succulent and gives a crispy coating. It is, however, essential that all poultry is cooked thoroughly. Test by piercing with a skewer in the thickest part—the juices should run clear when the meat is cooked. To avoid charred skins and raw centers, cook over coals that are not too hot. Place the rack about 4 inches above the coals. You should be able to hold your hand just above the rack for about 5 seconds; if it is too hot, reduce the temperature by raising the rack or spreading out the coals. However if the coals are not hot enough, the chicken will take too long to cook and will dry out.

Turkey can be a little dry, so baste it frequently with a glaze or marinade. Duckling has a stronger flavor and more fat than chicken or turkey, and it stands up very well to the barbecue treatment. Larger joints of poultry can be par-cooked in boiling water, the oven, or microwave, and finished on the barbecue.

Jerk Chicken

This is perhaps one of the best known Caribbean dishes. The "jerk" in the name refers to the hot spicy coating.

Serves 4

INGREDIENTS

4 chicken portions
1 bunch scallions, trimmed
1–2 Scotch Bonnet chilies, seeded
1 garlic clove

2-inch piece fresh ginger root, peeled and roughly chopped
$^1/_2$ tsp dried thyme
$^1/_2$ tsp paprika
$^1/_4$ tsp ground allspice

pinch ground cinnamon
pinch ground cloves
4 tbsp white wine vinegar
3 tbsp light soy sauce
pepper

1 Rinse the chicken portions and pat them dry on absorbent paper towels. Place them in a shallow dish.

2 Place the scallions, chilies, garlic, ginger, thyme, paprika, allspice, cinnamon, cloves, white wine vinegar, light soy sauce, and pepper to taste in a food processor and process to make a smooth mixture.

3 Pour the spicy mixture over the chicken. Turn the chicken portions so that they are well coated in the marinade. Transfer the chicken to the refrigerator and leave to marinate for up to 24 hours.

4 Remove the chicken from the marinade and broil over medium hot coals for about 30 minutes, turning the chicken over and basting occasionally with any remaining marinade, until it is cooked through.

5 Transfer the chicken portions to individual serving plates and serve at once.

COOK'S TIP

As Jamaican cuisine becomes increasingly popular, you will find jars of ready-made jerk marinade, which you can use when time is short. Allow the chicken to marinate for as long as possible for maximum flavor.

VARIATION

You can use milder chilies or even increase the amount of chili used.

Favorite Barbecued Chicken

These chicken wings are brushed with a simple barbecue glaze, which can be made in minutes, but the results are sure to delight everyone.

Serves 4

INGREDIENTS

8 chicken wings or 1 chicken cut into 8 portions	3 tbsp brown fruity sauce	1 tbsp olive oil
3 tbsp tomato paste	1 tbsp white wine vinegar	1 clove garlic, crushed (optional)
	1 tbsp clear honey	salad greens, to serve

1 Remove the skin from the chicken if you want to reduce the fat in the dish.

2 To make the barbecue glaze, place the tomato paste, brown fruity sauce, white wine vinegar, honey, oil, and garlic in a small bowl. Stir all of the ingredients together until they are thoroughly blended.

3 Brush the barbecue glaze over the chicken and broil over hot coals for 15–20 minutes. Turn the chicken portions over occasionally and baste frequently with the barbecue glaze. If the chicken begins to blacken before it is cooked thoroughly, raise the barbecue rack if possible or move the chicken to a cooler part of the barbecue in order to slow down the cooking.

4 Transfer the barbecued chicken to warm serving plates and serve immediately with fresh salad greens.

VARIATION

This barbecue glaze also makes a very good baste to brush over pork chops.

COOK'S TIP

When poultry is cooked over a very hot barbecue the heat immediately seals in all of the juices, leaving the meat succulent. For this reason you must make sure that the coals are hot enough before starting to cook.

Sticky Chicken Drumsticks

These drumsticks are always popular with children—make sure there are plenty of napkins for wiping sticky fingers or provide finger bowls with a slice of lemon.

Serves 10

INGREDIENTS

10 chicken drumsticks
4 tbsp fine-cut orange marmalade

1 tbsp Worcestershire sauce
grated rind and juice of $\frac{1}{2}$ orange
salt and pepper

TO SERVE:
cherry tomatoes
salad greens

1 Using a sharp knife, make 2–3 slashes in the flesh of each chicken drumstick.

2 Bring a large saucepan of water to a boil and add the chicken drumsticks. Cover the pan, return to a boil, and cook for 5–10 minutes. Remove the chicken and drain thoroughly.

3 Meanwhile, make the baste. Place the orange marmalade, Worcestershire sauce, orange rind and juice, and salt and pepper to taste in a small saucepan. Heat gently, stirring continuously, until the marmalade melts and all of the ingredients are well combined.

4 Generously brush the baste over the par-cooked chicken drumsticks and transfer them to the barbecue to complete cooking. Broil the drumsticks over hot coals for about 10 minutes, turning and basting frequently with the remaining baste.

5 Carefully thread 3 cherry tomatoes onto a skewer and transfer to the barbecue for 1–2 minutes.

6 Transfer the sticky chicken drumsticks to warm serving plates. Serve with the cherry tomato skewers and a selection of fresh salad greens.

COOK'S TIP

Par-cooking the chicken is an ideal way of making sure that it is cooked through without becoming overcooked and burned on the outside.

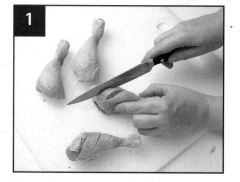

Chicken Tikka

Traditionally, chicken tikka is cooked in a clay tandoori oven, but it works well on the barbecue, too.

Makes 6

INGREDIENTS

4 skinless, boneless chicken breasts
$^1/_2$ tsp salt
4 tbsp lemon or lime juice

MARINADE:
$^2/_3$ cup unsweetened yogurt
2 cloves garlic, crushed

1-inch piece fresh ginger root, peeled and grated
1 tsp ground cumin
1 tsp chili powder
$^1/_2$ tsp ground coriander
$^1/_2$ tsp ground turmeric
oil or melted butter for brushing

SAUCE:
$^2/_3$ cup unsweetened yogurt
1 tsp mint sauce

1 Cut the chicken into 1-inch cubes. Sprinkle with the salt and the lemon or lime juice and let stand for about 10 minutes.

2 To make the marinade, combine the yogurt, garlic, ginger, and ground spices together in a small bowl until well mixed.

3 Thread the cubes of chicken onto skewers. Brush the marinade over the chicken. Cover and marinate in the refrigerator for at least 2 hours, preferably overnight.

4 Broil the chicken skewers over hot coals, brushing with oil or butter and turning frequently, for about 15 minutes, or until cooked through.

5 Meanwhile, combine the yogurt and mint to make the sauce. Serve the chicken skewers with the mint and yogurt sauce.

VARIATION

Use the marinade to coat chicken portions, such as drumsticks, rather than cubes of chicken, if you prefer. Broil over medium hot coals for 30–40 minutes, until the juices run clear when the chicken is pierced with a skewer.

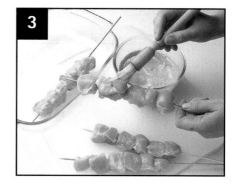

Indian Charred Chicken

*An Indian-influenced dish that is delicious served
with naan bread and a cucumber raita.*

Serves 4

INGREDIENTS

4 skinless, boneless chicken breasts
2 tbsp curry paste
1 tbsp sunflower oil
1 tbsp light muscovado sugar
1 tsp ground ginger
1/2 tsp ground cumin

TO SERVE:
naan bread
salad greens

CUCUMBER RAITA:
1/4 cucumber
salt
2/3 cup unsweetened yogurt
1/4 tsp chili powder

1 Place the chicken breasts between 2 sheets of baking parchment or plastic wrap. Pound them with the flat side of a meat mallet or with a rolling pin to flatten them.

2 Mix together the curry paste, oil, sugar, ginger, and cumin in a small bowl. Spread the mixture over both sides of the chicken and set aside until required.

3 To make the raita, peel the cucumber and scoop out the seeds with a spoon. Grate the cucumber flesh, sprinkle with salt, place in a strainer, and let stand for 10 minutes. Rinse off the salt and squeeze out any moisture by pressing the cucumber with the base of a glass or back of a spoon.

4 To make the raita, mix the cucumber with the yogurt and stir in the chili powder. Chill until required.

5 Transfer the chicken breasts to an oiled rack and broil over hot coals for about 10 minutes, turning once.

6 Warm the naan bread at the side of the barbecue. Serve the chicken with the naan bread and raita, and accompanied with fresh salad greens.

COOK'S TIP

*Flattening the chicken breasts
makes them thinner, so that they
cook more quickly.*

Cajun Spicy Chicken

*The Cajun spices are rubbed into the chicken, which is left to stand so that
the flavors have time to penetrate the flesh and develop.*

Serves 4

INGREDIENTS

4 chicken portions
1 clove garlic
1 tbsp light muscovado sugar
3 tbsp paprika

2 tsp cayenne pepper
1 tsp dried oregano
1 tsp dried sage
1 tsp dried thyme

4 tbsp sunflower oil
2 tbsp lemon juice
salt and pepper

1 Remove the skin from the chicken if you want to reduce the fat content. Using a sharp knife, make 2–3 slashes in the flesh of the chicken.

2 Cut the garlic clove in half and rub the cut surface over the chicken. Season the chicken portions with salt and pepper.

3 Mix together the sugar, spices, and dried herbs in a small bowl. Sprinkle over the chicken and rub into the flesh. Cover and let stand in the refrigerator for at least 2 hours.

4 Mix together the oil and lemon juice in a small bowl. Brush the mixture liberally over the chicken.

5 Broil the chicken over medium hot coals for about 30 minutes, turning and basting occasionally with the oil and lemon mixture.

6 Check that the chicken is cooked by piercing the thickest part with a skewer—the juices should run clear. Return the chicken to the barbecue to cook for a little longer if necessary.

7 Transfer the chicken to warm serving plates and serve at once.

VARIATION

This recipe also works well with pork. Rub the spiced mixture onto pork chops or side pork slices—they will taste delicious.

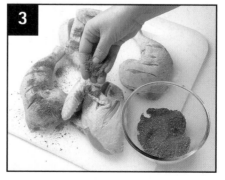

Spatchcock Baby Chicken with Garlic & Herbs

It is not difficult to spatchcock—open out—baby chickens, but it is the best way to cook whole birds on the barbecue.

Serves 2

INGREDIENTS

2 baby chickens, 1 pound each
6 tbsp butter
2 cloves garlic, crushed
2 tbsp chopped, mixed fresh herbs

BASTE:
4 tbsp olive oil
2 tbsp lemon juice
2 tbsp chopped, mixed herbs

salt and pepper

1 To open out each chicken, place each bird on its breast and use sharp scissors or poultry shears to cut along the length of the backbone. Open out the bird as much as possible and place it breast side up on a chopping board. Press down firmly on the breast bone to break it.

2 Mix together the butter, garlic, and herbs until well combined. Lift up the skin from the breast of each chicken. Divide the butter equally between the

2 chickens and spread over the breast under the skin.

3 Open out each bird. Thread 2 skewers diagonally through each bird to hold it flat.

4 Mix together the ingredients for the baste in a bowl.

5 Place the birds, bone side down, over medium hot coals and broil for 25 minutes, basting with the lemon and herb baste. Turn the birds over and

broil, skin side down, for 15 minutes, basting frequently, or until cooked through.

COOK'S TIP

Use a combination of whatever fresh herbs you have on hand. Thyme, rosemary, mint, oregano, parsley, or cilantro are all suitable. If you want to cook a whole chicken in this way, double the amount of baste and cook for 40–50 minutes.

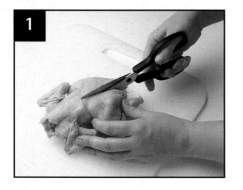

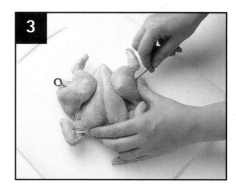

Sweet Maple Chicken

You can use any chicken portions for this recipe. Boned chicken thighs are economical for large barbecue parties, but you could also use wings or drumsticks.

Serves 6

INGREDIENTS

2 boned chicken thighs
5 tbsp maple syrup
1 tbsp superfine sugar
grated rind and juice of $^1/_2$ orange
2 tbsp ketchup

2 tsp Worcestershire sauce

TO GARNISH:
slices of orange
sprig of parsley

TO SERVE:
Italian bread, such as focaccia
salad greens
cherry tomatoes, quartered

1 Using a sharp knife, make 2–3 slashes in the flesh of the chicken. Place the chicken in a shallow, nonmetallic dish.

2 To make the marinade, mix together the maple syrup, sugar, orange rind and juice, ketchup, and Worcestershire sauce in a small bowl.

3 Pour the marinade over the chicken, tossing the chicken to coat thoroughly. Cover and chill in the refrigerator until required.

4 Remove the chicken from the marinade, reserving the marinade for basting.

5 Transfer the chicken to the barbecue and cook over hot coals for 20 minutes, turning the chicken and basting with the marinade frequently.

6 Transfer the chicken to serving plates and garnish with slices of orange and a sprig of parsley. Serve with Italian bread, fresh salad greens, and cherry tomatoes.

COOK'S TIP

If time is short, you can omit the marinating time. If you use chicken quarters, rather than the smaller thigh portions, parboil them for 10 minutes before brushing with the marinade and broiling on the barbecue.

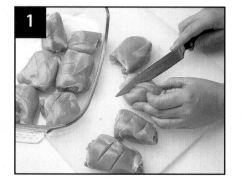

Chicken Skewers with Lemon & Cilantro

A tangy lemon yogurt is served with this tasty chicken dish.

Serves 4

INGREDIENTS

4 skinless, boneless chicken breasts	1¼ cups unsweetened yogurt	2 tbsp chopped, fresh cilantro
1 tsp ground coriander	1 lemon	oil for brushing
2 tsp lemon juice		salt and pepper

1 Cut the chicken into 1-inch pieces and place them in a shallow, nonmetallic dish.

2 Add the coriander, lemon juice, salt and pepper to taste, and 4 tbsp of the yogurt to the chicken and mix together until thoroughly combined. Cover and chill for at least 2 hours, preferably overnight.

3 To make the lemon yogurt, peel and finely chop the lemon, discarding any pits. Stir the lemon into the yogurt, together with the fresh cilantro. Chill in the refrigerator until required.

4 Thread the chicken pieces onto skewers. Brush the rack with oil and broil the chicken over hot coals for about 15 minutes, basting with the oil.

5 Transfer the chicken kabobs to warm serving plates and garnish with a sprig of fresh cilantro, lemon wedges, and fresh salad greens. Serve with the lemon yogurt.

VARIATION

These kabobs are delicious served on a bed of blanched spinach, which has been seasoned with salt, pepper, and nutmeg.

COOK'S TIP

Prepare the chicken the day before it is needed so that it can marinate overnight. This will allow the flavors to be fully absorbed.

Chicken Satay

This is an ideal sauce to accompany food cooked on the barbecue,
and it can be kept warm at the side of the rack.

Serves 4

INGREDIENTS

2 skinless, boneless chicken breasts

MARINADE:
4 tbsp sunflower oil
2 cloves garlic crushed
3 tbsp fresh, chopped cilantro
1 tbsp superfine sugar
$^1/_2$ tsp ground cumin

$^1/_2$ tsp ground coriander
1 tbsp soy sauce
1 red or green chili, seeded
salt and pepper

SAUCE:
2 tbsp sunflower oil
1 small onion, finely chopped

1 red or green chili, seeded
 and chopped
$^1/_2$ tsp ground coriander
$^1/_2$ tsp ground cumin
8 tbsp peanut butter
8 tbsp chicken stock or water
1 tbsp creamed coconut

1 Soak 8 wooden skewers in a large, shallow dish of cold water for at least 30 minutes. This process will prevent the skewers from burning during barbecuing.

2 Cut the chicken breasts lengthwise into 8 long strips. Thread the strips of chicken, accordion-style, onto the skewers and set aside while you make the marinade.

3 Place the ingredients for the marinade in a food processor and process until smooth.

4 Coat the chicken with the marinade paste, cover, and chill in the refrigerator for at least 2 hours.

5 To make the sauce, heat the oil in a small pan and sauté the onion and chili until they are

softened, but not browned. Stir in the spices and cook for 1 minute. Add the remaining sauce ingredients and cook the mixture gently for 5 minutes. Keep warm at the side of the barbecue.

6 Broil the chicken skewers over hot coals for about 10 minutes, basting with any remaining marinade. Serve with the warm sauce.

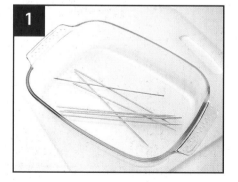

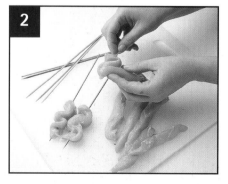

Thai-style Chicken Skewers

Here the chicken is marinated in a delicious aromatic sauce
before being threaded onto skewers.

Serves 4

INGREDIENTS

4 skinless, boneless chicken breasts
1 onion, peeled and cut into wedges
1 large red bell pepper, seeded
1 large yellow bell pepper seeded

12 kaffir lime leaves
2 tbsp sunflower oil
2 tbsp lime juice
tomato halves, to serve

MARINADE:
1 tbsp Thai red curry paste
$2/3$ cup canned coconut milk

1 To make the marinade, place the red curry paste in a small pan over medium heat and cook for 1 minute. Add half of the coconut milk to the pan and bring the mixture to a boil. Boil for 2–3 minutes, until the liquid has reduced by about two-thirds.

2 Remove the pan from the heat and stir in the remaining coconut milk. Set aside to cool.

3 Cut the chicken into 1-inch pieces. Stir the chicken into the cold marinade, cover, and chill for at least 2 hours.

4 Cut the onion into wedges and the bell peppers into 1-inch pieces.

5 Remove the chicken pieces from the marinade and thread them onto skewers, alternating the chicken with the vegetables and lime leaves.

6 Combine the oil and lime juice in a small bowl and brush the mixture over the kabobs. Broil the skewers over hot coals, turning and basting frequently with the oil and lime mixture, for 10–15 minutes, until the chicken is

cooked through. Broil the tomato halves on the barbecue and serve with the chicken skewers.

COOK'S TIP

Cooking the marinade first intensifies the flavor. It is important to allow the marinade to cool before adding the chicken, or bacteria may breed in the warm temperature. You will find fresh kaffir lime leaves in Asian food stores, but if these are unavailable, bay leaves can be used instead.

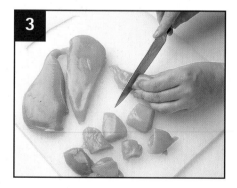

Sesame Chicken Brochettes with Cranberry Sauce

The cranberries give the sauce a lovely tart flavor. It can be served hot or cold.

Makes 8

INGREDIENTS

4 skinless, boneless chicken breasts
4 tbsp dry white wine
1 tbsp light muscovado sugar
2 tbsp sunflower oil
6¹/₂ tbsp sesame seeds
salt and pepper

TO SERVE:
boiled new potatoes
salad greens

SAUCE:
1¹/₂ cups cranberries
²/₃ cup cranberry juice drink
2 tbsp light muscovado sugar

1 Cut the chicken into 1-inch pieces. Stir together the wine, sugar, oil, and salt and pepper to taste in a large bowl. Add the chicken and toss to coat. Marinate in the refrigerator for at least 30 minutes, turning the chicken occasionally.

2 To make the sauce, place the ingredients in a small saucepan and bring slowly to a boil, stirring. Simmer gently for 5–10 minutes, until the cranberries are soft. Taste and add extra sugar if desired. Keep warm or chill, as required.

3 Remove the chicken pieces from the marinade with a slotted spoon. Thread the chicken pieces onto 8 skewers, spacing them slightly apart to ensure even cooking.

4 Broil on an oiled rack over hot coals for 4–5 minutes on each side, until just cooked. Brush several times with the marinade during cooking.

5 Remove the chicken skewers from the rack and roll in the sesame seeds. Return to the barbecue and cook for about 1 minute on each side or until the sesame seeds are toasted. Serve with the cranberry sauce, new potatoes, and salad greens.

VARIATION

Cranberry sauce goes well with all types of poultry. Try it with turkey or guinea fowl.

Chicken Skewers with Red Bell Pepper Sauce

These kabobs are rather special and are well worth the extra effort needed to prepare them.

Serves 4

INGREDIENTS

3 skinless, boneless chicken breasts
6 tbsp olive oil
4 tbsp lemon juice
$^1/_2$ small onion, grated
1 tbsp fresh, chopped sage
8 tbsp sage and onion stuffing mix

6 tbsp boiling water
2 green bell peppers, seeded

SAUCE:
1 tbsp olive oil

1 red bell pepper, seeded and
   finely chopped
1 small onion, finely chopped
pinch sugar
$7^1/_2$ ounce can chopped tomatoes

1 Cut the chicken into even-size pieces.

2 Mix the oil, lemon juice, grated onion, and sage and pour the mixture into a plastic bag. Add the chicken, seal the bag, and shake to coat the chicken. Marinate in the refrigerator for at least 30 minutes, shaking the bag occasionally.

3 Place the stuffing mix in a bowl and add the boiling water, stirring to mix well.

4 Cut each bell pepper into 6 strips, then blanch them in boiling water for 3–4 minutes, until softened. Drain and rinse in cold water, then drain again.

5 Form about 1 teaspoon of the stuffing mixture into a ball and roll it up in a strip of bell pepper. Repeat for the remaining stuffing mixture and bell pepper strips. Thread 3 bell pepper rolls onto each skewer alternately with pieces of chicken. Let chill.

6 To make the sauce, heat the oil in a small pan and sauté the red bell pepper and onion for 5 minutes. Add the sugar and tomatoes and simmer for about 5 minutes. Set aside and keep warm.

7 Broil the skewers on an oiled rack over hot coals, basting frequently with the remaining marinade, for about 15 minutes, until the chicken is cooked. Serve with the red bell pepper sauce.

Maryland Chicken Kabobs

A barbecue variation of the traditional dish,
Chicken Maryland. Serve with corn cobs (see page 198).

Makes 4

INGREDIENTS

8 chicken thighs, skinned and boned
1 tbsp white wine vinegar
1 tbsp lemon juice
1 tbsp corn syrup or clear honey
6 tbsp olive oil

1 clove garlic, crushed
4 slices bacon
2 bananas
salt and pepper

TO SERVE:
4 cooked corn cobs (see page 198)
mango chutney

1 Cut the chicken into bite-size pieces. Combine the vinegar, lemon juice, syrup or honey, oil, garlic, and salt and pepper to taste in a large bowl. Add the chicken pieces to the marinade and toss until the chicken is well coated. Cover and marinate in the refrigerator for 1–2 hours.

2 Stretch the bacon slices with the back of a knife and then cut each bacon slice in half. Cut the bananas into 1-inch lengths and brush them with lemon juice to prevent any discoloration.

3 Wrap a piece of bacon around each piece of banana.

4 Remove the chicken from the marinade, reserving the marinade for basting. Thread the chicken pieces, the bacon, and banana rolls alternately onto skewers.

5 Broil the kabobs over hot coals for about 8–10 minutes, until the chicken is completely cooked. Baste the kabobs with the reserved marinade and turn the skewers frequently.

6 Serve with corn cobs and mango chutney.

VARIATION

For a quick Maryland-style dish, omit the marinating time and cook the chicken thighs over hot coals for about 20 minutes, basting with the marinade. Broil the bananas in their skins alongside the chicken. Serve the bananas split open with a teaspoon of mango chutney.

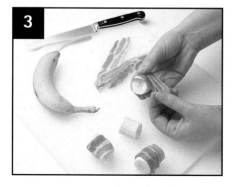

Turkey Steaks with Redcurrant Glaze

Prepare these steaks the day before they are needed and serve in
toasted Italian bread accompanied with crisp salad greens.

Serves 4

INGREDIENTS

¹/₃ cup redcurrant jelly
2 tbsp lime juice
4 tbsp olive oil
2 tbsp dry white wine

¹/₄ tsp ground ginger
pinch grated nutmeg
4 turkey breast steaks
salt and pepper

TO SERVE:
mixed salad greens
vinaigrette dressing
1 Italian loaf
cherry tomatoes

1 Put the redcurrant jelly and lime juice in a small pan and heat gently, stirring, until the jelly melts. Stir in the oil, wine, ginger, and nutmeg.

2 Place the turkey steaks in a shallow, nonmetallic dish and season with salt and pepper. Pour the redcurrant mixture on top, turning the meat so that it is well coated. Cover and chill in the refrigerator overnight.

3 Remove the turkey from the marinade, reserving the marinade for basting, and broil on an oiled rack over hot coals for about 4 minutes on each side. Baste the turkey steaks frequently with the reserved marinade.

4 Meanwhile, toss the salad greens in the vinaigrette dressing. Cut the Italian loaf in half lengthwise and place, cut side down, at the side of the barbecue. Broil until golden.

5 Cut each half of bread into 4 pieces. Serve the turkey steaks on top of salad greens and sandwiched between 2 pieces of bread.

VARIATION

Turkey and chicken escalopes are also ideal for cooking on the barbecue. Because they are thin, they cook through without burning on the outside. Leave them overnight in a marinade of your choice, or cook, basting with a little lemon juice and oil mixture, and season well.

Charbroiled Turkey with Cheesy Pockets

Wrapping bacon around the turkey helps to
keep the cheese enclosed in the pocket.

Serves 4

INGREDIENTS

4 turkey breast pieces, each about
    8 ounces
4 portions full-fat cheese (such as
    Bel Paese), $1/2$ ounce each

4 sage leaves or $1/2$ tsp dried sage
8 slices rindless fatty bacon
4 tbsp olive oil
2 tbsp lemon juice
salt and pepper

TO SERVE:
garlic bread
salad greens
cherry tomatoes

1 Carefully cut a pocket into the side of each turkey breast. Open out each breast a little and season inside with salt and pepper to taste.

2 Place a portion of cheese into each pocket, spreading it a little with a knife. Tuck a sage leaf into each pocket, or sprinkle with a little dried sage if you prefer.

3 Stretch the bacon out with the back of a knife. Wrap 2 pieces of bacon around each turkey breast, so that the pocket opening is completely covered.

4 Mix together the oil and lemon juice in a small bowl until well combined.

5 Broil the turkey over medium hot coals for about 10 minutes on each side, basting with the oil and lemon mixture frequently.

6 Place the garlic bread at the side of the barbecue and toast lightly.

7 Transfer the turkey to warm serving plates. Serve with the toasted garlic bread, salad greens, and a few cherry tomatoes.

VARIATION

You can vary the cheese you use to stuff the turkey—try grated mozzarella, or slices of brie or camembert. Also try placing 1 teaspoon of redcurrant jelly or cranberry sauce into each pocket instead of the sage.

COOK'S TIP

If you wish, use a toothpick to keep the turkey and bacon in place while they cook.

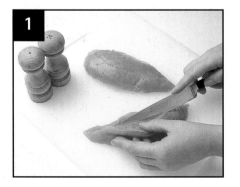

Spicy Turkey & Sausage Kabobs

Serve these tasty kabobs with fresh bread such as ciabatta, focaccia, or French bread.

Makes 8

INGREDIENTS

turkey breast fillet, about 12 ounces
10 $1/2$ ounces chorizo or other
   seasoned pork sausage
1 eating apple
1 tbsp lemon juice
8 bay leaves

BASTE:
6 tbsp olive oil
2 cloves garlic, crushed
1 red chili, seeded and chopped
salt and pepper

1 To make the baste, place the oil, garlic, chili, and salt and pepper to taste in a small screw-top jar and shake well to combine. Let stand for 1 hour for the garlic and chili to flavor the oil.

2 Cut the turkey into 1-inch pieces. Cut the sausage into 1-inch lengths.

3 Cut the apple into chunks and remove the core. Toss the apple in lemon juice to prevent discoloration.

4 Thread the turkey and sausage pieces onto 8 skewers, alternating with the apple chunks and bay leaves.

5 Broil the kabobs over hot coals for about 15 minutes, or until the turkey is thoroughly cooked. Turn the kabobs and baste them frequently with the flavored oil.

6 Transfer the kabobs to warm individual serving plates and serve at once.

COOK'S TIP

The flavored oil used in this recipe can be used to baste any broiled meat, fish, or vegetables. It will give plain foods a subtle chili flavor and will keep in the refrigerator for about 2 weeks.

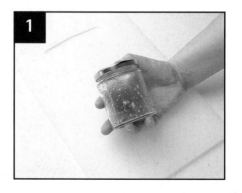

Sherried Chicken Liver Brochettes

*Economical and flavorsome, these tasty kabobs
make an ideal light lunch.*

Serves 4

INGREDIENTS

14 ounces chicken liver, trimmed
  and cleaned
3 slices bacon
1 Italian loaf or small French bread
8 ounces baby spinach, washed

MARINADE:
$^2/_3$ cup dry sherry
4 tbsp olive oil
1 tsp wholegrain mustard
salt and pepper

MUSTARD MAYONNAISE:
8 tbsp mayonnaise
1 tsp wholegrain mustard

1 Cut the chicken liver into 2-inch pieces. To make the marinade, combine the sherry, oil, mustard, and salt and pepper to taste in a shallow dish. Add the chicken liver to the marinade and toss until well coated. Marinate in the refrigerator for 3–4 hours.

2 To make the mayonnaise, stir the mustard into the mayonnaise and chill.

3 Stretch out the bacon with the back of a knife and cut each slice into 2. Remove the chicken liver from the marinade, reserving the marinade for basting. Wrap the bacon around half of the chicken liver pieces. Thread the bacon and chicken liver rolls and the plain chicken liver pieces alternately onto 6 presoaked wooden skewers.

4 Broil the skewers over hot coals for 10–12 minutes, turning and basting with the reserved marinade frequently.

5 Meanwhile, cut the bread into 6 pieces and toast the cut sides on the barbecue until they are golden brown.

6 To serve, top the toasted bread with spinach leaves and place the kabobs on top. Spoon the mustard mayonnaise on top and serve immediately.

COOK'S TIP

Take care not to overcook the chicken livers or they will become tough. They should be firm to the touch and just pink inside.

Citrus Duckling Skewers

The tartness of citrus fruit goes well with the rich meat of duckling.

Serves 6

INGREDIENTS

3 skinless, boneless duckling breasts
1 small red onion, cut into wedges
1 small eggplant, cut into cubes

lime and lemon wedges, to
  garnish (optional)

MARINADE:
grated rind and juice of 1 lemon
grated rind and juice of 1 lime

grated rind and juice of 1 orange
1 clove garlic, crushed
1 tsp dried oregano
2 tbsp olive oil
dash of Tabasco sauce

1 Cut the duckling into bite-size pieces and place them in a nonmetallic bowl, together with the prepared red onion and eggplant cubes.

2 To make the marinade, place the lemon, lime and orange rinds and juices, garlic, oregano, oil, and Tabasco sauce in a screw-top jar and shake until combined.

3 Pour the marinade over the duckling and vegetables and toss to coat. Marinate in the refrigerator for 30 minutes.

4 Remove the duckling and vegetables from the marinade, reserving the marinade for basting, and thread them onto skewers.

5 Broil the skewers on an oiled rack over medium hot coals, turning and basting frequently with the reserved marinade, for 15–20 minutes, until the meat is cooked through.

6 Transfer to a serving plate and serve the kabobs garnished with lemon and lime wedges for squeezing, if using.

COOK'S TIP

For more zing add 1 teaspoon of chili sauce to the marinade. The meat can be marinated for several hours, but it is best to marinate the vegetables separately for only about 30 minutes.

Sesame Orange Duckling

*Moist and flavorful, this dish is reminiscent of duck
à la orange, but the flavor is even better.*

Serves 4

INGREDIENTS

4 tbsp soy sauce
2 tbsp fine-cut marmalade
2 tbsp orange juice
2 cloves garlic, crushed

$^1/_2$-inch piece fresh ginger
  root, grated
1 tbsp sherry vinegar
4 duckling portions
2 oranges, sliced

4 tbsp sesame seeds

TO SERVE:
salad greens
fresh herbs

1 Mix together the soy sauce, marmalade, orange juice, garlic, ginger, and vinegar in a small bowl until well combined.

2 Trim away any excess fat from the duckling portions.

3 Place the duckling portions in a shallow, nonmetallic dish and add the orange mixture. Cover and marinate in the refrigerator for at least 2 hours.

4 Divide most of the orange slices among 4 double-thickness pieces of kitchen foil,

reserving some orange slices to serve. Place a duckling portion on top of the oranges and pour some of the marinade over each portion. Fold over the foil to enclose the duckling completely.

5 Cook over hot coals for about 40 minutes or until the meat is just cooked.

6 Remove the foil packets from the heat and sprinkle the skin of the duckling with the sesame seeds. Place the duckling, skin side down, directly on the oiled rack over the hot coals and broil for a

further 5 minutes, until the skin is crisp. Serve with the reserved orange slices, salad greens and fresh herbs.

COOK'S TIP

Cooking the duckling in foil packets keeps the meat deliciously moist and means that all the flavor of the marinade is retained. If you prefer, you can omit the foil and cook them directly on the rack. Turn and baste frequently until cooked. Sprinkle with sesame seeds for the last few minutes of cooking.

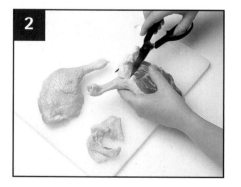

Barbecued Duckling

*The sweet, spicy marinade used in this recipe gives the duckling
a subtle flavor of the East.*

Serves 4

INGREDIENTS

3 cloves garlic, crushed
²/₃ cup light soy sauce
5 tbsp light muscovado sugar

1-inch piece fresh ginger root, grated
1 tbsp chopped, fresh cilantro

1 tsp five-spice powder
4 duckling breasts
sprig of fresh cilantro,
   to garnish

1 To make the marinade, mix together the garlic, soy sauce, sugar, grated ginger, chopped cilantro, and five-spice powder in a small bowl until well combined.

2 Place the duckling breasts in a shallow, nonmetallic dish and pour the marinade on top. Carefully turn the duckling breasts so that they are fully coated with the marinade on both sides.

3 Cover the bowl with plastic wrap and marinate in the refrigerator for 1–6 hours, turning the duckling once or twice so that the marinade is fully absorbed.

4 Remove the duckling from the marinade, reserving the marinade for basting.

5 Broil the duckling breasts over hot coals for about 20–30 minutes, turning and frequently basting with the reserved marinade.

6 Cut the duckling into slices and transfer to warm serving plates. Serve garnished with a sprig of fresh cilantro.

COOK'S TIP

Duckling is quite a fatty meat, so there is no need to add oil to the marinade. However, you must remember to oil the barbecue rack to prevent the duckling from sticking to it. It is a good idea to oil the barbecue rack well away from the barbecue to avoid any danger of a flare-up.

Glazed Duckling with Pineapple Salsa

A salsa is a cross between a sauce and a relish. Salsas are easy to prepare and will liven up all kinds of simple broiled meats.

Serves 4

INGREDIENTS

2 tbsp Dijon mustard
1 tsp paprika
$\frac{1}{2}$ tsp ground ginger
$\frac{1}{2}$ tsp ground nutmeg
2 tbsp dark muscovado sugar

2 duckling halves
salad greens, to serve

SALSA:
8 ounce can pineapple in
  natural juice
2 tbsp dark muscovado sugar
1 small red onion, finely chopped
1 red chili, seeded and chopped

1 To make the salsa, drain the pineapple, reserving 2 tbsp of the juice. Finely chop the pineapple flesh.

2 Place the pineapple, reserved juice, sugar, onion, and chili in a bowl and mix well. Let stand for at least 1 hour for the flavors to develop fully.

3 Meanwhile, mix together the mustard, paprika, ginger, nutmeg, and sugar. Spread the mixture evenly over the skin of the duckling halves.

4 Broil the duckling, skin side up, over hot coals for about 30 minutes. Turn the duckling over and broil for 10–15 minutes, or until the duckling halves are cooked through.

5 Serve with fresh salad greens and the salsa.

COOK'S TIP

You could place the ducklings in a rectangular foil tray to protect the delicate flesh on the barbecue.

VARIATION

Use canned apricots or peaches to make the salsa for a tasty alternative. The salsa is also delicious served with pork, lamb, or chicken.

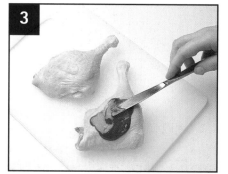

Meat

Most people think of meat when they think of barbecues, and even the simplest chop tastes wonderful when cooked on the barbecue. Add marinades or bastes, and you have the most appetizing meal you can possibly imagine.

The following recipes include suggestions for all of your favorite cuts of meat, as well as new approaches to those barbecue favorites, burgers and sausages. Don't be afraid of experimenting and mixing the bastes and marinades with different cuts and types of meat.

If you are having an impromptu barbecue, choose recipes with a baste, although, if time permits, marinating meat not only adds flavor, but helps to ensure that the meat is tender. Trim any excess fat from the meat so that it does not drip onto the coals, causing them to flare up—keep a water spray handy just in case.

Beef and lamb can be served pink in the center, but you must make sure that pork is cooked thoroughly. Test it with a skewer to see if the juices run clear.

Beef Toppers

Hamburgers need never be dull when they are accompanied with one of these tasty toppings.

Makes 6

INGREDIENTS

1 pound 9 ounces lean ground beef
1 onion, finely chopped
2 tbsp Worcestershire sauce
salt and pepper
sesame rolls, toasted, to serve

SAVORY MUSHROOMS:
2 cups sliced button mushrooms
1 tbsp soy sauce
1 tbsp Worcestershire sauce

GUACAMOLE:
1 avocado
1 clove garlic
1 tbsp lemon juice

1 tbsp tomato relish

BARBECUE SAUCE:
3 tbsp brown fruity sauce
3 tbsp ketchup
1 tsp wholegrain mustard
1 tbsp clear honey

1 Choose one or all of the following toppings. To make the savory mushrooms, combine all of the ingredients and set aside for at least 30 minutes.

2 To make the guacamole topping, peel, pit, and mash the avocado. Mix the avocado with the garlic, lemon juice, and tomato relish until well combined and chill in the refrigerator until required.

3 To make the barbecue sauce, combine all of the ingredients and chill in the refrigerator until required.

4 To make the burgers, mix together the ground beef, onion, Worcestershire sauce, and salt and pepper to taste until well combined. Divide into 6 portions and mold each into a neat patty, about 1/2 inch thick. Chill for at least 30 minutes.

5 Broil over hot coals for 5-10 minutes on each side. Serve the burgers in the rolls, with the topping spooned on top.

COOK'S TIP

A hamburger is only as good as the meat you use, so choose the best quality you can. For a more economical hamburger add 1 cup fresh breadcrumbs.

Beef Teriyaki

*This Japanese-style teriyaki sauce complements beef,
but it can also be used to accompany chicken or salmon.*

Serves 4

INGREDIENTS

1 pound extra thin beef steaks
8 scallions, trimmed and cut into
   short lengths
1 yellow bell pepper, seeded and cut
   into chunks
salad greens, to serve

SAUCE:
1 tsp cornstarch
2 tbsp dry sherry
2 tbsp white wine vinegar
3 tbsp soy sauce

1 tbsp dark muscovado sugar
1 clove garlic, crushed
$1/2$ tsp ground cinnamon
$1/2$ tsp ground ginger

1 Place the meat in a shallow, nonmetallic dish.

2 To make the sauce, combine the cornstarch with the sherry, then stir in the remaining sauce ingredients. Pour the sauce over the meat and marinate in the refrigerator for at least 2 hours.

3 Remove the meat from the sauce and set aside. Pour the sauce into a small saucepan.

4 Cut the meat into thin strips and thread these, accordion-style, onto presoaked wooden skewers, alternating each strip of meat with the prepared pieces of yellow bell pepper and scallion.

5 Gently heat the sauce until it is just simmering, stirring it from time to time so that it does not stick to the bottom of the pan.

6 Broil the kabobs over hot coals for 5–8 minutes, turning and basting the beef and vegetables occasionally with the reserved teriyaki sauce.

7 Arrange the skewers on serving plates and pour the remaining sauce over the kabobs. Serve with salad greens.

COOK'S TIP

If you are short on time, omit the marinating, but the flavor will not permeate the meat as well.

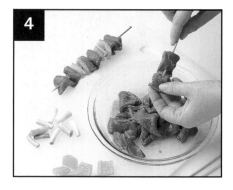

Boozy Beef Steaks

A simple marinade gives plain steaks a fabulous flavor with very little effort.

Serves

INGREDIENTS

4 beef steaks	1 tbsp dark muscovado sugar	TO SERVE:
4 tbsp whiskey or brandy	pepper	garlic bread
2 tbsp soy sauce	fresh sprig of parsley, to garnish	slices of tomato

1 Make a few cuts in the edge of fat on each steak. This will stop the meat curling as it cooks.

2 Place the meat in a shallow, nonmetallic dish.

3 Combine the whiskey or brandy, soy sauce, sugar, and pepper to taste in a small bowl, stirring until the sugar dissolves. Pour the mixture over the steak. Cover and marinate in the refrigerator for at least 2 hours.

4 Broil the meat over hot coals, searing the surface of the steak over the hottest part of the barbecue for about 2 minutes on each side.

5 Move the meat to an area of the barbecue with slightly less intense heat and cook for a further 4–10 minutes on each side, depending on how well done you like your steaks. Test the meat is cooked by inserting the tip of a knife into it—the juices will run from red, when the meat is still rare, to clear, as it becomes well cooked.

6 Lightly barbecue the slices of tomato for 1–2 minutes.

7 Transfer the meat and the tomatoes to warm serving plates. Garnish with a sprig of fresh parsley and serve with garlic bread.

COOK'S TIP

Steaks are ideal for cooking on the barbecue. Choose a good quality steak, such as fillet, club, T-bone, or porterhouse, with a light marbling of fat to prevent the meat from becoming too dry as it cooks. Quick-fry steaks can also be used, but these have to be pounded with a meat mallet to flatten and tenderize the meat.

Mexican Steaks with Avocado Salsa

Coated in Mexican spices and served with a refreshing avocado salsa,
these steaks will pep up your barbecue fare.

Serves 4

INGREDIENTS

4 beef steaks
3 tbsp sunflower oil
1/2 red onion, grated
1 red chili, seeded and finely chopped
1 clove garlic, crushed
1 tbsp chopped, fresh cilantro
1/2 tsp dried oregano
1 tsp ground cumin

AVOCADO SALSA:
1 ripe avocado
grated rind and juice of 1 lime
1 tbsp sunflower oil
1/2 red onion, finely chopped
1 red chili, seeded and finely chopped
1 tbsp chopped, fresh cilantro
salt and pepper

1 Make a few cuts in the edge of fat around each steak to prevent the meat from curling as it cooks. Place the meat in a shallow, nonmetallic dish.

2 Mix the oil, onion, chili, garlic, cilantro, oregano, and cumin in a small bowl until well combined. Pour the marinade over the steaks, turning the meat so that it is well coated. Marinate in the refrigerator for 1–2 hours.

3 To make the salsa, halve the avocado and remove the pit. Peel and cut the flesh into small dice. Combine the avocado with the lime rind and juice, oil, onion, chili, cilantro, and salt and pepper to taste and mix well. Cover and chill in the refrigerator until required.

4 Broil the steaks on an oiled rack over hot coals for 6–12 minutes on each side.

5 Serve the steaks accompanied with the avocado salsa.

VARIATION

The avocado salsa can also be served with chicken. Reduce the amount of chili if you want a milder flavor. If fresh chilies are not available, look for jars of ground chilies, which are a good substitute.

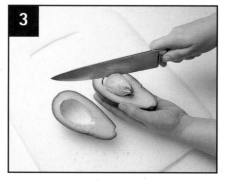

Barbecue Steaks with Red Onion Marmalade

Far from being sweet, this marmalade is a delicious savory relish.

Serves 4

INGREDIENTS

4 beef loin steaks
2 tsp wholegrain mustard
2 tbsp sunflower oil
grated rind and juice of $^1/_2$ orange
salt and pepper

cooked new potatoes, to serve

RED ONION MARMALADE:
2 tbsp olive oil
1 pound red onions, cut into rings

$^3/_4$ cup red wine
rind of 1 orange, grated
1 tbsp superfine sugar

1 To make the marmalade, place the olive oil and onions in a saucepan and sauté gently for 5–10 minutes, until the onions are just softened and are beginning to turn golden-brown—do not let them overcook.

2 Add the wine, orange rind, and sugar to the pan and simmer for 10–15 minutes until the onions are tender and most of the liquid has evaporated. Let cool, then season with salt and pepper to taste.

3 Make a few cuts in the edge of fat around each steak to prevent the meat from curling as it cooks.

4 Using a knife, spread each steak with a little of the mustard and season with salt and pepper to taste.

5 Mix together the oil and the orange juice and rind in a small bowl, and use this mixture to baste the steaks occasionally during cooking.

6 Broil the steaks over hot coals, searing the meat over the hottest part of the barbecue for 2 minutes on each side, basting occasionally with the orange mixture. Move the meat to an area with slightly less intense heat and cook, basting occasionally, for 4–10 minutes on each side, depending on how well done you like your steaks.

7 Transfer the steaks to plates and serve with the red onion marmalade and new potatoes.

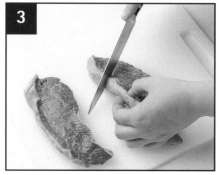

Surf & Turf Kabobs

This dish originated in Australia. The name refers to the shrimp from the sea—the "surf"—and the meat from the land—the "turf."

Makes 6

INGREDIENTS

1 pound sirloin steak
18 raw shrimp

MARINADE:
5 tbsp oyster sauce
1 tbsp soy sauce

3 tbsp lemon juice
4 tbsp sunflower oil

1 Cut the steak into 24 even-size pieces and place the meat in a nonmetallic dish.

2 Peel the shrimp, leaving the tails attached, as this makes them look attractive.

3 To make the marinade, combine the oyster sauce, soy sauce, lemon juice, and sunflower oil in a small bowl. Pour the mixture over the meat and marinate for 15 minutes.

4 Add the shrimp to the marinade, toss to coat, and marinate for 5 minutes.

5 Remove the meat and shrimp from the marinade, reserving the marinade for basting. Thread the meat onto metal or presoaked wooden skewers, alternating the steak with the shrimp. (Presoaking wooden skewers helps to prevent them from burning as the meat is cooking.)

6 Broil the kabobs over hot coals for 5–10 minutes, basting with the reserved marinade and turning frequently.

7 Transfer the kabobs to warm serving plates and serve immediately.

VARIATION

Other shellfish, such as lobster and crab, can be added to the skewers. These kabobs are also delicious marinated in, and basted with, an herb, garlic, and oil marinade.

Beef, Tomato, & Olive Kabobs

These kabobs have a Mediterranean flavor. The sweetness of the tomatoes and the sharpness of the olives makes them rather tempting.

Serves 8

INGREDIENTS

1 pound sirloin steak
16 cherry tomatoes
16 large green olives, pitted
Italian bread, to serve

BASTE:
4 tbsp olive oil

1 tbsp sherry vinegar
1 clove garlic, crushed
salt and freshly ground black pepper

FRESH TOMATO RELISH:
1 tbsp olive oil
1/2 red onion, finely chopped

1 clove garlic, chopped
6 plum tomatoes, seeded, skinned,
   and chopped
2 pitted green olives, sliced
1 tbsp chopped, fresh parsley
1 tbsp lemon juice

1 Trim any fat from the beef and cut the meat into about 24 even-size pieces.

2 Thread the meat onto 8 skewers, alternating it with cherry tomatoes and olives.

3 To make the baste, combine the oil, vinegar, garlic, and salt and pepper to taste in a bowl.

4 To make the relish, heat the oil in a small pan and sauté the onion and garlic for 3–4 minutes, until softened. Add the tomatoes and olives and cook for 2–3 minutes, until the tomatoes are softened. Stir in the parsley and lemon juice and season with salt and pepper to taste. Set aside and keep warm or chill.

5 Broil the skewers on an oiled rack over hot coals for 5–10 minutes, basting and turning frequently. Serve with the tomato relish and slices of Italian bread.

COOK'S TIP

The kabobs, baste, and relish can be prepared several hours in advance, avoiding the need for any last-minute rush. For a simple meal, serve with crusty fresh bread and a mixed salad.

Beef with Mushrooms

Choose thick steaks for this dish—it will be easier to cut the pockets in the side of each one.

Serves 4

INGREDIENTS

4 steaks, fillet or sirloin
4 tbsp butter
1–2 cloves garlic, crushed

5 ¹/₂ ounces mixed exotic
mushrooms
2 tbsp chopped, fresh parsley

TO SERVE:
salad greens
cherry tomatoes, halved

1 Place the steaks on a chopping board and using a sharp knife, cut a pocket into the side of each steak.

2 To make the stuffing, heat the butter in a skillet, add the garlic, and sauté gently for about 1 minute.

3 Add the mushrooms to the skillet and sauté gently for 4–6 minutes until tender. Stir in the parsley.

4 Divide the mushroom mixture into 4 and insert a portion into the pocket of each steak. Seal the pocket closed with a toothpick. If preparing ahead, allow the mixture to cool before stuffing the steaks.

5 Broil the steaks over hot coals, searing the meat over the hottest part of the barbecue for about 2 minutes on each side. Move the steaks to an area with slightly less intense heat and barbecue for a further 4–10 minutes on each side, depending on how well done you like your steaks.

6 Transfer the steaks to serving plates and remove the toothpicks. Serve with salad greens and cherry tomatoes.

COOK'S TIP

Exotic mushrooms, such as shiitake, oyster, and chanterelle, are now readily available in supermarkets.

Meatball Brochettes

Children will love these tasty meatballs on a skewer, which are economical and easy to make.

Makes 8

INGREDIENTS

⅛ cup cracked wheat
12 ounces lean ground beef
1 onion, very finely
   chopped (optional)

1 tbsp ketchup
1 tbsp brown fruity sauce
1 tbsp chopped, fresh parsley
beaten egg, to bind

8 cherry tomatoes
8 button mushrooms
oil, to baste
8 hot dog buns, to serve

1 Place the cracked wheat in a bowl and cover with boiling water. Leave to soak for 20 minutes, or until softened. Drain thoroughly and set aside to cool.

2 Place the wheat, ground beef, onion (if using), ketchup, brown sauce, and parsley together in a mixing bowl and mix well. Add a little beaten egg if necessary to bind the mixture together.

3 Using your hands, shape the meat mixture into 18 even-size balls. Chill in the refrigerator for 30 minutes.

4 Carefully thread the meatballs onto 8 presoaked wooden skewers, alternating them with the cherry tomatoes and button mushrooms.

5 Brush the kabobs with a little oil and broil over hot coals for about 10 minutes, turning occasionally and brushing with a little more oil if necessary.

6 Transfer the kabobs to warm serving plates. Cut open each of the hot dog buns and push the meat and vegetables off the skewers into the open rolls to serve, if you wish.

COOK'S TIP

The cracked wheat "stretches" the beef, making this a cheap and cheerful meal. It also produces a less dense meatball with a nutty texture that children often like.

Charbroiled Venison Steaks

*Venison has a good strong flavor, which makes it an ideal meat
to barbecue. Marinate overnight to tenderize the meat.*

Serves 4

INGREDIENTS

4 venison steaks	few sprigs fresh parsley	salt and pepper
$2/3$ cup red wine	2 sprigs fresh thyme	
2 tbsp sunflower oil	1 bay leaf	TO SERVE:
1 tbsp red wine vinegar	1 tsp superfine sugar	baked potatoes
1 onion, chopped	$1/2$ tsp mild mustard	salad greens and cherry tomatoes

1 Place the venison steaks in a shallow, nonmetallic dish.

2 Combine the wine, oil, wine vinegar, onion, fresh parsley, thyme, bay leaf, sugar, mustard, and salt and pepper to taste in a screw-top jar and shake vigorously until well combined. Alternatively, using a fork, whisk the ingredients together in a bowl.

3 Pour the marinade mixture over the venison, turn the steaks, cover, and marinate in the refrigerator overnight. Turn the steaks over in the mixture occasionally, so that the meat is well coated.

4 Broil the venison steaks over hot coals, searing the meat over the hottest part of the barbecue for about 2 minutes on each side.

5 Move the meat to an area with slightly less intense heat and barbecue for a further 4–10 minutes on each side, depending on how well done you like your steaks. Test if the meat is cooked by inserting the tip of a knife into the meat—the juices will run from red, when the meat is still rare, to clear, as the meat becomes well cooked.

6 Serve with baked potatoes, salad greens, and tomatoes.

COOK'S TIP

Farmed venison is available all year round. Look for it in the meat section of the supermarket or order it from an independent butcher. This dish is also delicious when served with red onion marmalade (see page 104).

Lamb Burgers with Mint & Pine Nuts

These tasty burgers have a Greek flavor. Serve them in the traditional soft roll or in pita bread.

Serves 4

INGREDIENTS

1 pound lean ground lamb
1 small onion, finely chopped
1/4 cup pine nuts

2 tbsp chopped, fresh mint
salt and pepper

TO SERVE:
4 pita breads or soft rolls
1/8 cup feta cheese
salad greens

1 Place the ground lamb, chopped onion, pine nuts, fresh mint, and salt and pepper to taste in a large bowl and mix together until all the ingredients are thoroughly combined.

2 Using your hands, divide the mixture into 4 and shape the portions into round burgers, pressing the mixture together well. Chill in the refrigerator for 30 minutes.

3 Broil the burgers over hot coals for 4–5 minutes on each side, turning once, until the juices run clear.

4 Warm the pita breads at the side of the barbecue or toast the rolls.

5 Crumble the feta cheese into small pieces and set aside until required.

6 Line the pita bread or rolls with the salad greens. Sandwich the burgers between the bread or rolls, and top with the crumbled feta cheese.

COOK'S TIP

If you do not have any fresh mint, use 1–2 teaspoons of mint sauce, which has a much fresher taste than dried mint. Chill the burgers in the refrigerator before cooking them, so that they become firmer and are far less likely to fall apart.

Butterfly Chops with Redcurrant Glaze

A butterfly chop is a double chop cut across the saddle. They make an attractive cut, but you can use single chops if you prefer.

Serves 4

INGREDIENTS

4 tbsp redcurrant jelly
2 tbsp raspberry vinegar
1/2 tsp dried rosemary
1 clove garlic, crushed

1 tbsp sunflower oil
4 butterfly lamb chops or 8 loin lamb chops

4 baby eggplant
oil, for basting

1 To make the glaze, combine the redcurrant jelly, vinegar, rosemary, garlic, and oil in a small pan and heat, stirring occasionally, until the jelly melts and the ingredients are well blended.

2 Broil the chops over hot coals for 5 minutes on each side.

3 Cut each baby eggplant in half and brush the cut sides liberally with oil.

4 Broil the eggplant halves alongside the lamb for about 3–4 minutes on each side, or until completely cooked through. Set them aside and keep warm until required.

5 Brush the glaze over the chops and broil the meat for a further 5 minutes on each side, basting frequently, until the meat is cooked. Keep the redcurrant glaze warm at the side of the barbecue.

6 Transfer the lamb and eggplant halves to warm serving plates and pour the remaining redcurrant glaze on top. Serve at once.

VARIATION

You can use other lamb cuts for this dish—leg chops or rib chops are ideal. The redcurrant glaze also goes well with chicken; parboil or microwave chicken drumsticks, then brush them with the redcurrant glaze and finish off cooking on the barbecue.

Lamb with a Spice Crust

Boned, cushion shoulder roast or neck slices are tender cuts that are not too thick and are therefore ideal for cooking on the barbecue.

Serves 4

INGREDIENTS

1 tbsp olive oil
2 tbsp light muscovado sugar
2 tbsp wholegrain mustard
1 tbsp horseradish sauce

1 tbsp all-purpose flour
12 ounces boned cushion shoulder or
  neck slices of lamb
salt and pepper

TO SERVE:
coleslaw
slices of tomato

1 Combine the oil, sugar, mustard, horseradish sauce, flour, and salt and pepper to taste in a shallow, nonmetallic dish until they are well mixed.

2 Roll the lamb in the spice mixture until well coated.

3 Lightly oil one or two pieces of foil or a large, double thickness of foil. Place the lamb on the foil and wrap it up so that the meat is completely enclosed.

4 Place the foil packet over hot coals for 30 minutes, turning the packet over occasionally.

5 Open the foil, spoon the cooking juices over the lamb, and continue to cook for a further 10-15 minutes, or until cooked through.

6 Transfer the lamb to a warm serving plate and remove the foil. Cut the lamb into thick slices and serve with coleslaw and a few slices of tomato.

COOK'S TIP

Lamb is naturally fatter than beef, which makes it a good choice for cooking on the barbecue.

COOK'S TIP

If preferred, the lamb can be completely removed from the foil for the second part of the cooking. Cook the lamb directly over the coals for a smokier barbecue flavor, basting with extra oil if necessary.

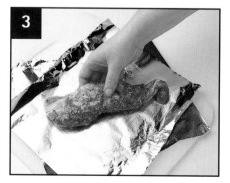

Kibbeh

*This Lebanese dish is similar to the Turkish kofte and the Indian kofta,
but the spices used to flavor the meat are quite different.*

Makes 8

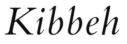

INGREDIENTS

¹/₂ cup couscous
1 small onion
12 ounces lean ground lamb
¹/₂ tsp ground cinnamon

¹/₄ tsp cayenne
4 tsp ground allspice
salad greens and onion rings,
    to serve

BASTE:
2 tbsp ketchup
2 tbsp sunflower oil

1 Place the couscous in a large bowl, cover with cold water and let stand for 30 minutes, or until the couscous has swelled and softened. Alternatively, soak the couscous according to the instructions on the packet.

2 Drain the couscous through a strainer and squeeze out as much moisture as you can.

3 Put the onion in a food processor and chop finely. Add the lamb and process briefly to chop the ground meat further. Alternatively, grate the onion before mixing with the lamb.

4 Combine the couscous, lamb, and spices and mix well. Divide the mixture into 8 equal-size portions. Press and shape the mixture around 8 skewers, pressing the mixture together firmly so that it holds its shape. Chill in the refrigerator for 30 minutes.

5 To make the baste, combine the oil and ketchup.

6 Broil the kibbeh over hot coals for 10–15 minutes, turning and basting frequently. Serve with barbecued onion rings and salad greens.

VARIATION

The spicy baste used in this recipe also works well with barbecued vegetables.

COOK'S TIP

Putting the ground lamb through the food processor chops it further and helps the mixture hold together better. Adding couscous to a ground meat mixture "stretches" the meat, making the dish very economical to make. You can add it to other types of meat and use it to make kabobs or burgers.

Barbecued Lamb Ribs

These sweet and spicy lamb ribs are best eaten with your fingers.
Make sure there are plenty of napkins available.

Serves 4

INGREDIENTS

breast of lamb, about 1 pound
   9 ounces
3 tbsp sweet chutney
4 tbsp ketchup

2 tbsp cider vinegar
2 tsp Worcestershire sauce
2 tsp mild mustard
1 tbsp light muscovado sugar

TO SERVE:
salad greens
cherry tomatoes

1 Using a sharp knife, cut between the ribs of the breast of lamb to divide it into slightly smaller pieces.

2 Bring a large saucepan of water to a boil, add the lamb and parboil for about 5 minutes. Remove the meat from the water and pat dry thoroughly with paper towels.

3 Combine the sweet chutney, ketchup, cider vinegar, Worcestershire sauce, mustard, and sugar in a shallow, nonmetallic dish to make a smooth sauce.

4 Using a sharp knife, cut the lamb into individual ribs. Add the ribs to the sauce and toss until well coated.

5 Remove the ribs from the sauce, reserving the remaining sauce for basting.

6 Broil the ribs over hot coals for 10-15 minutes, turning and basting frequently with the reserved sauce.

7 Transfer the ribs to warm serving plates. Serve immediately with salad greens and cherry tomatoes.

VARIATION

Use side of pork strips if you prefer and, as with the lamb, parboil the pork to remove some of the excess fat from the meat.

COOK'S TIP

If you are short on time, look for ready-prepared lamb ribs—they are widely available in most large supermarkets.

Butterfly Lamb with Balsamic Vinegar & Mint

The appearance of the leg of lamb as it is opened out to cook on the barbecue gives this dish its name.

Serves 4

INGREDIENTS

boned leg of lamb, about 4 pounds	4 tbsp chopped, fresh mint	TO SERVE:
8 tbsp balsamic vinegar	2 cloves garlic, crushed	broiled vegetables
grated rind and juice of 1 lemon	2 tbsp light muscovado sugar	salad greens
$^2/_3$ cup sunflower oil	salt and pepper	

1 Open out the boned leg of lamb so that its shape resembles a butterfly. Thread 2–3 skewers through the meat to make it easier to turn when cooking on the barbecue.

2 Combine the balsamic vinegar, lemon rind and juice, oil, mint, garlic, sugar, and salt and pepper to taste in a nonmetallic dish that is large enough to hold the lamb.

3 Place the lamb in the dish and turn it over a few times so that the meat is coated on both sides with the marinade. Marinate in the refrigerator for at least 6 hours or preferably overnight, turning occasionally.

4 Remove the lamb from the marinade and reserve the liquid for basting.

5 Place the rack about 6 inches above the coals and barbecue the lamb for about 30 minutes on each side, turning once and basting frequently with the reserved marinade.

6 Transfer the lamb to a chopping board and remove the skewers. Cut the lamb into slices across the grain and serve with broiled vegetables and crisp salad greens.

COOK'S TIP

If you prefer, cook the lamb for half the cooking time in a preheated oven at 350°F, then finish off cooking on the barbecue.

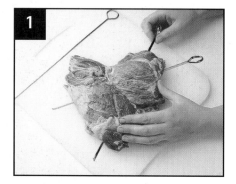

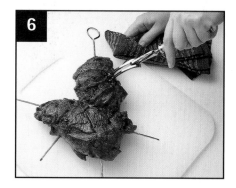

Red Wine Lamb Skewers

*Use the best quality red wine you can afford. Instead of using fresh herbs,
add a bouquet garni to the marinade, if you prefer.*

Makes 4

INGREDIENTS

1 pound lean lamb
12 button onions or shallots
12 button mushrooms
salad greens and cherry tomatoes,
    to serve

MARINADE:
$^2/_3$ cup red wine
4 tbsp olive oil
2 tbsp brandy (optional)

1 onion, sliced
1 bay leaf
sprig of fresh thyme
2 sprigs fresh parsley

1 Carefully trim away any excess fat from the lamb. Cut the lamb into large pieces.

2 To make the marinade, combine the wine, oil, brandy (if using), onion, bay leaf, thyme, and parsley in a nonmetallic dish.

3 Add the meat to the dish and toss to coat the meat thoroughly in the marinade. Cover the dish and marinate the lamb in the refrigerator for at least 2 hours or preferably overnight.

4 Bring a pan of water to a rolling boil, drop in the unpeeled button onions, and blanch them for 3 minutes. Drain and rinse the onions under cold water, and then drain again. Trim the onions and remove their skins, which will now slip off easily.

5 Remove the meat from the marinade, reserving the liquid for basting. Thread the meat onto skewers, alternating with the button onions and mushrooms.

6 Broil the kabobs over hot coals for 8–10 minutes, turning and basting the meat and vegetables with the reserved marinade a few times.

7 Transfer the lamb kabobs to a warm serving plate and serve with fresh salad greens and cherry tomatoes.

VARIATION

This recipe also works well with beef. Bacon rolls can also be added to the skewers, if you like.

Moroccan Lamb Kabobs

Marinated in Moroccan spices, these kabobs have a mild spicy flavor.
Add the chili if you like a little zip to your meat.

Makes 4

INGREDIENTS

1 pound lean lamb
1 lemon
1 red onion
4 small zucchini
couscous, to serve (see Cook's Tip)

MARINADE:
grated rind and juice of 1 lemon
2 tbsp olive oil
1 clove garlic, crushed
1 red chili, sliced (optional)

1 tsp ground cinnamon
1 tsp ground ginger
1/2 tsp ground cumin
1/2 tsp ground coriander

1 Cut the lamb into large, even-size chunks.

2 To make the marinade, combine the lemon rind and juice, oil, garlic, chili (if using), ground cinnamon, ginger, cumin, and coriander in a large nonmetallic dish.

3 Add the meat to the marinade, tossing to coat the meat completely. Cover and marinate in the refrigerator for a minimum of 2 hours or preferably overnight.

4 Cut the lemon into 8 pieces. Cut the onion into wedges, then separate each wedge into 2 pieces.

5 Using a canelle knife or potato peeler, cut thin strips of peel from the zucchini, then cut the zucchini into chunks.

6 Remove the meat from the marinade, reserving the liquid for basting. Thread the meat onto skewers alternating with the onion wedges, lemon pieces, and chunks of zucchini.

7 Broil over hot coals for 8–10 minutes, turning and basting with the reserved marinade. Serve on a bed of couscous (see Cook's Tip).

COOK'S TIP

Serve these kabobs with couscous or tabouleh. Allowing 1/3 cup couscous per person, soak the couscous in cold water for about 20 minutes, until the grains have softened. Drain and steam for 10 minutes, or until piping hot.

Shish Kabobs

The name of this dish derives from the Turkish words sis *(skewer) and* kebap *(roast meat).*
A favorite in restaurants, these kabobs are easy to make at home.

Makes 4

INGREDIENTS

1 pound lean lamb
1 red onion, cut into wedges
1 green bell pepper, seeded

MARINADE:
1 onion

4 tbsp olive oil
grated rind and juice of $1/2$ lemon
1 clove garlic, crushed
$1/2$ tsp dried oregano
$1/2$tsp dried thyme

TO SERVE:
4 pita breads
2 tomatoes, sliced
few crisp lettuce leaves, shredded
chili sauce (optional)

1 Cut the lamb into large, even-size chunks.

2 To make the marinade, grate the onion or chop it very finely in a food processor. Remove the juice by squeezing the onion between two plates set over a small bowl to collect the juice.

3 Combine the onion juice with the remaining marinade ingredients in a nonmetallic dish and add the meat. Toss the meat in the marinade, cover, and marinate in the refrigerator for at least 2 hours or overnight.

4 Divide the onion wedges into 2. Cut the bell peppers into chunks.

5 Remove the meat from the marinade, reserving the liquid for basting. Thread the meat onto skewers, alternating with the onion and bell peppers. Broil over hot coals for 8–10 minutes, turning and basting frequently with the reserved marinade.

6 Split open the pita breads and fill with a little lettuce. Serve the kabobs in the bread, pushing the meat and vegetables off the skewers as you do so. Top with tomatoes and chili sauce.

VARIATION

These kabobs are delicious served with saffron-flavored rice and a mixed salad. For easy saffron rice, simply use saffron stock cubes when cooking the rice.

Lamb Cutlets with Rosemary

A classic combination of flavors, this dish would make a perfect Sunday lunch.
Serve with tomato and onion salad and baked potatoes.

Serves 4

INGREDIENTS

8 lamb cutlets
5 tbsp olive oil
2 tbsp lemon juice
1 clove garlic, crushed
$1/2$ tsp lemon pepper
salt
8 sprigs rosemary

baked potatoes, to serve

SALAD:
4 tomatoes, sliced
4 scallions, sliced diagonally

DRESSING:
2 tbsp olive oil
1 tbsp lemon juice
1 clove garlic, chopped
$1/4$ tsp fresh rosemary, finely chopped

1 Trim the lamb cutlets by cutting away the flesh with a sharp knife to expose the tips of the bones.

2 Place the oil, lemon juice, garlic, lemon pepper, and salt in a shallow, nonmetallic dish and whisk with a fork to combine.

3 Lay the sprigs of rosemary in the dish and place the lamb on top. Marinate for at least 1 hour in the refrigerator, turning the lamb cutlets once.

4 Remove the cutlets from the marinade and wrap a little foil around the bones to stop them from burning.

5 Place the sprigs of rosemary on the rack and place the lamb on top. Broil for about 10–15 minutes, turning once.

6 Meanwhile, make the salad and dressing. Arrange the tomatoes on a serving dish and scatter the scallions on top. Place all the ingredients for the dressing in a screw-top jar, shake well, and pour over the salad. Serve with the broiled lamb cutlets and baked potatoes.

COOK'S TIP

Choose medium to small baking potatoes if you want to cook the potatoes on the barbecue. Scrub them well, prick with a fork, and wrap in buttered foil. Bury them in the hot coals and barbecue for 50–60 minutes.

Lamb with Mango & Chili

*These lamb chops really pack a punch when they are
served with a hot spicy mango relish.*

Serves 4

INGREDIENTS

4 loin of lamb or English chops
4 tbsp mango chutney
2 tsp chili sauce
broiled vegetables, to serve

SPICY MANGO RELISH:
1 ripe mango
2 tbsp cider vinegar

2 tbsp light muscovado sugar
$^1/_2$ tsp ground cinnamon
$^1/_2$ tsp ground ginger

1 To make the spicy mango relish, cut the mango lengthwise down both sides of the large, flat pit and discard the pit. Peel the mango and cut the flesh into even-size chunks.

2 Place the cider vinegar, sugar, cinnamon, and ginger in a small pan and heat gently, stirring continuously, until the sugar has completely dissolved.

3 Stir the mango into the mixture in the pan and cook gently at the side of the barbecue for about 5 minutes, or until the mango is soft.

4 Barbecue the chops on an oiled rack for about 4 minutes on each side.

5 Combine the mango chutney and chili sauce in a small bowl and brush the glaze over both sides of the chops.

6 Continue to barbecue for a further 2–5 minutes on each side, until the lamb is cooked, turning and basting frequently with the mango chutney and chili glaze.

7 Serve with broiled vegetables and the spicy mango relish.

VARIATION

The spicy mango relish can also be served cold. Simmer the combined ingredients for 5 minutes, then remove from the heat and allow to cool. Chill in the refrigerator until required. You can also use the mango chutney and chili glaze on other cuts of lamb or on pork chops.

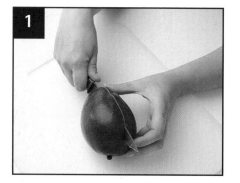

Indian Kofta

Lean ground lamb is mixed with curry paste to produce a flavorful Indian-style kabob, which is served with a refreshing tomato sambal.

Makes 8

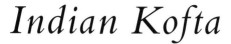

INGREDIENTS

1 small onion
1 pound minced lamb
2 tbsp curry paste
2 tbsp unsweetened yogurt
oil, to baste
sprigs of fresh cilantro,
   to garnish

TOMATO SAMBAL:
3 tomatoes, seeded and diced
pinch of ground coriander
pinch of ground cumin
2 tsp chopped, fresh cilantro
salt and pepper

TO SERVE:
poppadoms
chutney

1 Put the onion in a food processor and chop finely. Add the lamb and process briefly to chop the ground meat further. Chopping the lamb again will help the meat mixture to hold together during cooking. If you do not have a food processor, grate the onion finely before mixing it with the ground lamb.

2 Add the curry paste and yogurt and mix well. Divide the mixture into 8 equal portions.

3 Press and shape the mixture into 8 sausage shapes and push each one onto a skewer, pressing the mixture together firmly so that it holds its shape. Chill the kabobs in the refrigerator for at least 30 minutes or until required.

4 To make the tomato sambal, mix together the tomatoes, coriander, cumin, chopped cilantro, and salt and pepper to taste in a bowl. Let stand for at least 30 minutes for the flavors to combine.

5 Broil the kabobs on an oiled rack over hot coals for 10–15 minutes, turning frequently. Baste the kabobs with a little oil if required.

6 Transfer to serving plates and garnish with fresh cilantro. Serve accompanied with poppadoms, chutney, and the tomato sambal.

Sweet Lamb Fillet

*Lamb fillet, enhanced by a sweet and spicy glaze, is cooked
in a foil packet for deliciously moist results.*

Serves 4

INGREDIENTS

2 fillets of lamb, 8 ounces each	5 tbsp apple juice	salt and pepper
1 tbsp olive oil	3 tbsp smooth apple sauce	salad greens, croûtons, and fresh
1/2 onion, finely chopped	1 tbsp light muscovado sugar	crusty bread, to serve
1 clove garlic, crushed	1 tbsp ketchup	
1-inch piece fresh ginger root, grated	1/2 tsp mild mustard	

1 Place the lamb fillets on a large piece of double thickness foil. Season with salt and pepper to taste.

2 Heat the oil in a small pan and sauté the onion and garlic for 2–3 minutes, until softened, but not browned. Stir in the grated ginger and cook for 1 minute, stirring occasionally.

3 Stir in the apple juice, apple sauce, sugar, ketchup, and mustard and bring to a boil. Boil rapidly for about 10 minutes, until reduced by half. Stir the mixture occasionally so that it does not burn and stick to the pan.

4 Brush half of the sauce over the lamb, then wrap up the lamb in the foil to completely enclose it. Cook the lamb over hot coals for about 25 minutes, turning the packet over from time to time.

5 Open the foil packets and brush the lamb with some of the sauce. Continue to barbecue for a further 15–20 minutes, or until cooked through and tender.

6 Place the lamb on a chopping board, remove the foil, and cut into thick slices. Transfer to serving plates and spoon the remaining sauce on top. Serve with salad greens, croûtons, and fresh crusty bread.

COOK'S TIP

If you prefer, you can cook the lamb for the first part of the cooking time in a preheated oven at 350°F. Place the foil packet in an ovenproof dish to avoid any leaking.

Lamb Noisettes with Tomato Salsa

Here, the lamb is served with a fragrant tomato side dish. If you like your meals
a little spicy, add chili sauce to both the salsa and the marinade.

Serves 4

INGREDIENTS

8 lamb noisettes
4 basil leaves
2 tbsp olive oil
grated rind and juice of ¹/₂ lime
salt and pepper

sprig of fresh basil, to garnish
salad greens, to serve

SALSA:
6 tomatoes

4 basil leaves
8 stuffed green olives
1 tbsp lime juice
pinch of superfine sugar

1 Place the lamb noisettes in a shallow, nonmetallic dish. Tear the basil leaves into pieces and scatter them over the lamb.

2 Drizzle the oil and lime juice over the lamb and add the lime rind. Season with salt and pepper to taste. Cover and marinate in the refrigerator for at least 1 hour or preferably overnight.

3 To make the salsa, skin the tomatoes by cutting a small cross at the stem. Drop the tomatoes into boiling water for

about 30 seconds, remove with a slotted spoon, and then peel off the skins.

4 Cut the tomatoes in half, then scoop out the seeds, and discard them. Cut the tomato flesh into large dice. Tear the basil leaves into pieces. Chop the olives. Mix together the tomatoes, basil, olives, lime juice, and sugar in a bowl and set aside for at least 1 hour or until required.

5 Remove the lamb from the marinade, reserving the marinade for basting. Broil over

hot coals for 10–15 minutes, turning once and basting with the reserved marinade.

6 Garnish with a sprig of basil and serve with the tomato salsa and salad greens.

COOK'S TIP

Green olives are picked and processed before they have ripened. Some are pickled and stuffed, usually with a little red pimiento or a sliver of almond. Use either in this recipe and chop the stuffing.

Caribbean Pork

*Serve these tasty marinated pork chops with a coconut-flavored savory rice
and accompanied with Spicy Sweet Potato Slices (page 178).*

Serves 4

INGREDIENTS

4 pork loin chops
4 tbsp dark muscovado sugar
4 tbsp orange or pineapple juice
2 tbsp Jamaican rum
1 tbsp shredded coconut
1/2 tsp ground cinnamon

mixed salad greens, to serve

COCONUT RICE:
1 generous cup Basmati rice
2 cups water
2/3 cup coconut milk

4 tbsp raisins
4 tbsp roasted peanuts or
   cashew nuts
salt and pepper
2 tbsp shredded coconut, toasted

1 Trim any excess fat from the pork and place the chops in a shallow, nonmetallic dish.

2 Combine the sugar, fruit juice, rum, coconut, and cinnamon in a bowl, stirring until the sugar dissolves. Pour the mixture over the pork and marinate in the refrigerator for at least 2 hours or preferably overnight.

3 Remove the pork from the marinade, reserving the liquid for basting. Broil over hot coals for 15–20 minutes, basting with the marinade.

4 Meanwhile, make the coconut rice. Rinse the rice under cold water, place it in a pan with the water and coconut milk, and bring gently to a boil. Stir, cover, and reduce the heat. Simmer gently for 12 minutes, or until the rice is tender and the liquid has been absorbed. Fluff up with a fork.

5 Stir the raisins and nuts into the rice, season with salt and pepper to taste, and sprinkle with the coconut. Transfer the pork and rice to warm serving plates and serve with the mixed salad greens.

VARIATION

These pork chops are delicious served with barbecued pineapple slices. Sprinkle the pineapple with dark muscovado sugar and cinnamon. Broil over hot coals for 5 minutes, turning once, until piping hot.

Ham Steaks with Spicy Apple Rings

This dish is quick to prepare because there is no marinating involved. Ham has a good, strong flavor and cooks well on the barbecue.

Serves 4

INGREDIENTS

4 ham steaks, about 6 ounces each
1–2 tsp wholegrain mustard
1 tbsp honey
2 tbsp lemon juice
1 tbsp sunflower oil

APPLE RINGS:
2 green eating apples
2 tsp raw sugar
$^{1}/_{4}$ tsp ground nutmeg
$^{1}/_{4}$ tsp ground cinnamon

$^{1}/_{4}$ tsp ground allspice
1–2 tbsp melted butter

1 Using a pair of scissors, make a few cuts around the edges of the ham steaks to prevent them from curling up as they cook. Spread a little wholegrain mustard over the steaks.

2 Mix together the honey, lemon juice, and oil in a bowl.

3 To prepare the apple rings, core the apples and cut them into thick slices. Mix the sugar with the spices and press the apple slices in the mixture until well coated on both sides.

4 Broil the steaks over hot coals for 3–4 minutes on each side, basting with the honey and lemon mixture to prevent the meat from drying out during cooking.

5 Brush the apple slices with a little melted butter and broil alongside the meat for about 3–4 minutes, turning once and brushing with melted butter as they cook.

6 Transfer the ham steaks to warm serving plates with the apple slices as a garnish.

COOK'S TIP

Ham can be a little salty. If you have time, soak the steaks in cold water for 30–60 minutes before cooking—this process will remove the excess salt.

VARIATION

Pineapple rings can also be cooked in the same way as the apple rings for a delicious alternative garnish to this dish.

Pork & Apple Skewers with Mustard

*Flavored with mustard and served with a mustard sauce, these kabobs
make an ideal lunch or they can be served as part of a large barbecue spread.*

Makes 4

INGREDIENTS

1 pound pork tenderloin	2 tsp wholegrain mustard	MUSTARD SAUCE:
2 eating apples	2 tsp Dijon mustard	1 tbsp wholegrain mustard
a little lemon juice	2 tbsp apple or orange juice	1 tsp Dijon mustard
1 lemon	2 tbsp sunflower oil	6 tbsp light cream
	crusty brown bread, to serve	

1 To make the mustard sauce, combine the wholegrain and Dijon mustards in a small bowl and slowly blend in the cream. Set aside while you prepare the pork and apple skewers.

2 Cut the pork tenderloin into bite-size pieces and set aside until required.

3 Core the apples, then cut them into thick wedges. Toss the apple wedges in a little lemon juice—this will prevent any discoloration. Cut the lemon into slices.

4 Thread the pork, apple, and lemon slices alternately onto 4 skewers.

5 Mix together the mustards, fruit juice, and oil in a bowl until well combined. Brush the mixture over the kabobs and broil over hot coals for 10–15 minutes, turning and basting frequently with the mustard marinade.

6 Transfer the kabobs to warm serving plates and spoon a little of the mustard sauce on top. Serve hot with fresh, crusty brown bread, if wished.

COOK'S TIP

There are many varieties of mustard available, including English mustard, which is very hot, Dijon, which is milder, and wholegrain mustard, which contains whole mustard seeds. Mustards flavored with other ingredients, such as honey or chili, are also available. It is well worth keeping some in the cupboard.

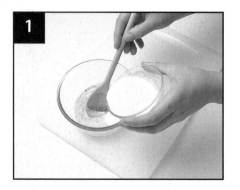

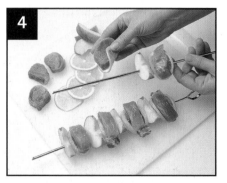

Pork Ribs with Plum Sauce

Pork ribs are always very popular at barbecues, and you can flavor them with a number of spicy bastes. This slightly sweet version has a delicious Chinese flavor.

Serves 4–6

INGREDIENTS

2 pounds pork spareribs
2 tbsp sunflower oil
1 tsp sesame oil
2 cloves garlic, crushed
1-inch piece fresh ginger root, grated

$^2/_3$ cup plum sauce
2 tbsp dry sherry
2 tbsp hoisin sauce
2 tbsp soy sauce
4–6 scallions, to garnish (optional)

1 To prepare the garnish, trim the scallions to about 3 inches long. Slice both ends into thin strips, leaving the onion intact in the center.

2 Put the scallions into a bowl of iced water for at least 30 minutes, until the ends start to curl up. Leave them in the water and set aside until required for the garnish.

3 If you buy the spareribs in a single piece, cut them into individual ribs. Bring a large pan of water to a boil and add the ribs. Cook for 5 minutes, then drain them thoroughly.

4 Heat the oils together in a pan, add the garlic and ginger, and cook gently for 1–2 minutes to bring out the flavor. Stir in the plum sauce, sherry, hoisin sauce, and soy sauce and heat gently until warmed through.

5 Brush the sauce over the pork ribs. Broil over hot coals for 5–10 minutes, then move the ribs to a cooler part of the barbecue.

Broil for a further 15–20 minutes, basting with the remaining sauce. Transfer the ribs to warm serving plates, garnish with the scallion brushes, if using, and serve hot.

COOK'S TIP

Parboiling the ribs removes excess fat, which helps prevent the ribs from splitting during cooking. Do not be put off by the large quantity—there is only a little meat on each, but they are quite cheap to buy.

Fruity Pork Skewers

Prunes and apricots bring color and flavor to these tasty pork kabobs.

Makes 4

INGREDIENTS

4 boneless pork loin steaks
8 ready-to-eat prunes
8 ready-to-eat dried apricots
4 bay leaves

slices of orange and lemon,
   to garnish

MARINADE:
4 tbsp orange juice
2 tbsp olive oil
1 tsp ground bay leaves
salt and pepper

1 Trim the visible fat from the pork and cut the meat into even-size chunks.

2 Place the pork in a shallow, nonmetallic dish and add the prunes and apricots.

3 To make the marinade, mix together the orange juice, oil, bay leaves, and salt and pepper to taste in a bowl.

4 Pour the marinade over the pork and fruit and toss until well coated. Marinate in the refrigerator for at least 1 hour or preferably overnight.

5 Soak 4 wooden skewers in cold water to prevent them from catching fire on the barbecue during cooking.

6 Remove the pork and fruit from the marinade, using a slotted spoon, reserving the marinade for basting. Thread the pork and fruit onto the skewers, alternating with the bay leaves.

7 Broil the skewers on an oiled rack over medium hot coals for 10–15 minutes, turning and frequently basting with the reserved marinade, or until the pork is cooked through.

8 Transfer the pork and fruit skewers to warm serving plates. Garnish with slices of orange and lemon and serve hot.

COOK'S TIP

Pork should always be thoroughly cooked, but take care not to overcook it, as the meat can become rather dry. Always add oil to a marinade for pork. If the meat is cooking too quickly, raise the rack or move the meat to a cooler part of the barbecue.

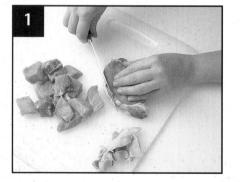

Spicy Pork Ribs

There are many ways of serving barbecued ribs.
This spicy sauce is based on a traditional Southern recipe.

Serves 4–6

INGREDIENTS

2 pounds pork spareribs
²/₃ cup sieved tomatoes
2 tbsp red wine vinegar
2 tbsp dark muscovado sugar

1 clove garlic, crushed
1 tsp dried thyme
¹/₂ tsp dried rosemary
1 tsp chili sauce

red chilies, to garnish (optional)
mixed salad greens, to serve

1 If you buy the spareribs in a single piece, carefully cut them into individual ribs using a very sharp knife.

2 Bring a large pan of water to a boil and add the pork ribs. Cook the ribs for 10 minutes, then drain them thoroughly. Place the ribs in a large, shallow, nonmetallic dish.

3 To make the spicy sauce, combine the sieved tomatoes, red wine vinegar, sugar, garlic, dried thyme, dried rosemary, and chili sauce in a bowl until thoroughly blended.

4 Pour the sauce over the pork ribs and toss to coat on all sides. Marinate in the refrigerator for 1 hour.

5 Remove the ribs from the sauce, reserving the sauce for basting. Broil the ribs over hot coals for 5–10 minutes, then move them to a cooler part of the barbecue. Cook for a further 15–20 minutes, turning and basting with the remaining sauce.

6 Transfer the ribs to warm serving plates and garnish with the red chilies (if using). Serve with the mixed salad greens.

COOK'S TIP

For authentic Southern-style ribs make sure you buy pork spareribs and not rib chops. Pork spareribs are often sold cut into individual ribs, but it is quite easy to cut between the ribs with a sharp knife if you cannot obtain them already separated.

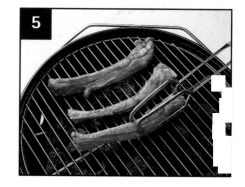

Ham & Pineapple Kabobs

This traditional combination of flavors always works well on the barbecue.

Makes 4

INGREDIENTS

1 pound thick ham steak
15 ounce can pineapple chunks, in natural juice
8 ounces firm brie, chilled

2 tbsp sunflower oil
1 clove garlic, crushed
1 tbsp lemon juice
$1/2$ tsp ground nutmeg

$1/4$ tsp ground cloves
pepper
cooked rice, to serve

1 Cut the ham into even-size chunks.

2 Place the ham in a pan of boiling water and simmer for 5 minutes.

3 Drain the pineapple pieces and reserve 3 tbsp of the juice. Cut the chilled cheese into large chunks.

4 To make the baste, combine the pineapple juice, oil, garlic, lemon juice, nutmeg, cloves, and pepper to taste in a small screw-top jar and shake until well combined. Set aside until required.

5 Remove the ham from the pan with a slotted spoon. Thread the ham chunks onto skewers, alternating with the pineapple pieces and the chunks of cheese.

6 Broil the kabobs over warm coals, turning and basting frequently with the oil and pineapple juice mixture, for 2–4 minutes on each side. Broil the kabobs until the pineapple and ham are hot and the cheese is just beginning to melt.

7 Serve the kabobs on a bed of cooked rice.

COOK'S TIP

Cook the skewers on the barbecue just long enough to reheat the ham and to warm the pineapple. Take care not to overcook the kabobs or you will end up with a sticky and unappetizing mess—the cheese should only just begin to melt.

VARIATION

Add cubes of a hard cheese, such as Swiss or Gouda, instead of the brie, if you prefer.

Honey-glazed Pork Chops

*The addition of freshly grated ginger gives a delicious
tang to the honey-flavored glaze.*

Serves 4

INGREDIENTS

4 lean pork loin chops
4 tbsp clear honey
1 tbsp dry sherry

4 tbsp orange juice
2 tbsp olive oil
1-inch piece fresh ginger root, grated
salt and pepper

1 Season the pork chops with salt and pepper to taste. Set aside while you make the glaze.

2 To make the glaze, place the honey, sherry, orange juice, oil, and ginger in a small pan and heat gently, stirring continuously, until all of the ingredients are well blended.

3 Broil the chops on an oiled rack over hot coals for about 5 minutes on each side.

4 Brush the chops with the glaze and broil for a further 2–4 minutes on each side, basting frequently with the glaze.

5 Transfer the chops to warm serving plates and serve hot.

VARIATION

This recipe works equally well with lamb chops and with chicken portions, such as thighs or drumsticks. Broil the meat in exactly the same way as in this recipe, basting frequently with the honey glaze—the result will be just as delicious!

COOK'S TIP

To give the recipe a little more punch, stir $1/2$ teaspoon of chili sauce or 1 tablespoon of wholegrain mustard into the basting glaze.

Sausages with Barbecue Sauce

Although there is much more to barbecues than sausages, they can make a welcome appearance from time to time. This delicious sauce is a wonderful excuse for including them again.

Serves 4

INGREDIENTS

2 tbsp sunflower oil
1 large onion, chopped
2 cloves garlic, chopped
8 ounce can chopped tomatoes
1 tbsp Worcestershire sauce

2 tbsp brown fruity sauce
2 tbsp light muscovado sugar
4 tbsp white wine vinegar
1/2 tsp mild chili powder
1/4 tsp mustard powder

dash of Tabasco sauce
1 pound sausages
salt and pepper
hot dog buns, to serve

1 To make the sauce, heat the oil in a small pan and sauté the onion and garlic for 4–5 minutes, until softened and just beginning to brown.

2 Add the tomatoes, Worcestershire sauce, brown fruity sauce, sugar, wine vinegar, chili powder, mustard powder, Tabasco sauce, and salt and pepper to taste and bring to a boil.

3 Reduce the heat and simmer gently for 10–15 minutes, until the sauce begins to thicken slightly. Stir occasionally so that the sauce does not burn and stick to the bottom of the pan. Set the sauce aside and keep warm until required.

4 Broil the sausages over hot coals for 10–15 minutes, turning frequently. Do not prick them with a fork or the juices and fat will run out and cause the barbecue to flare.

5 Put the sausages in the hot dog buns and serve with the barbecue sauce.

COOK'S TIP

Choose any well-flavored sausages for this recipe. German wurst sausages are a good choice, as are English Cumberland sausages, which are also available in a coil (secure the coil with skewers so that it does not unravel as it cooks). Venison sausages have a good, gamey flavor and taste wonderful cooked on the barbecue.

Tangy Pork Tenderloin

Barbecued in a packet of foil, this tasty pork tenderloin
is served with a tangy orange sauce.

Serves 4

INGREDIENTS

14 ounces pork tenderloin
3 tbsp orange marmalade
grated rind and juice of 1 orange
1 tbsp white wine vinegar
dash of Tabasco sauce
salt and pepper

SAUCE:
1 tbsp olive oil
1 small onion, chopped
1 small green bell pepper, seeded and
  thinly sliced
1 tbsp cornstarch

$^2/_3$ cup orange juice

TO SERVE:
cooked rice
mixed salad greens

1 Place a large piece of double-thickness foil in a shallow dish. Put the pork tenderloin in the center of the foil and season.

2 Heat the marmalade, orange rind and juice, vinegar, and Tabasco sauce in a small pan, stirring until the marmalade melts and the ingredients combine.

3 Pour the mixture over the pork and wrap the meat in foil, making sure that the packet is well sealed so that the juices

cannot run out. Place over hot coals and broil for about 25 minutes, turning the packet occasionally.

4 To make the sauce, heat the oil and cook the onion for 2–3 minutes, until softened. Add the bell pepper and cook for 3–4 minutes until it is just tender.

5 Remove the pork from the foil and place on the rack. Pour the cooking juices into the pan containing the sauce.

6 Broil the pork for a further 10–20 minutes, turning, until cooked through and golden on the outside.

7 In a small bowl, mix the cornstarch with a little orange juice to form a paste. Add to the sauce with the remaining cooking juices. Cook, stirring, until the sauce thickens.

8 Cut the pork into slices and transfer to plates. Spoon the sauce over the pork and serve.

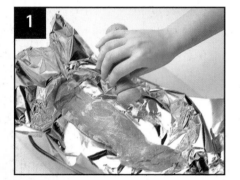

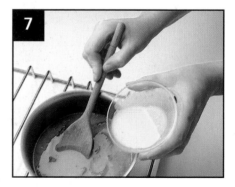

Pork & Sage Kabobs

The ground pork mixture is shaped into meatballs and threaded onto skewers.
They have a delicious, slightly sweet flavor that is popular with children.

Makes 12

INGREDIENTS

1 pound ground pork
1/2 cup fresh breadcrumbs
1 small onion, very finely chopped
1 tbsp fresh sage, chopped
2 tbsp apple sauce
1/4 tsp ground nutmeg

salt and pepper

BASTE:
3 tbsp olive oil
1 tbsp lemon juice

TO SERVE:
6 small pita breads
mixed salad greens
6 tbsp thick, unsweetened yogurt

1 Place the pork in a mixing bowl, together with the breadcrumbs, onion, sage, apple sauce, nutmeg, and salt and pepper to taste. Mix until the ingredients are well combined.

2 Using your hands, shape the mixture into small balls, about the size of large marbles, and chill in the refrigerator for at least 30 minutes.

3 Meanwhile, soak 12 small wooden skewers in cold water for at least 30 minutes. Thread the meatballs onto the skewers.

4 To make the baste, mix together the oil and lemon juice in a small bowl, whisking with a fork until it is well blended.

5 Broil the kabobs over hot coals for 8–10 minutes, turning and basting frequently with the lemon and oil mixture, until the meat is golden and cooked through.

6 Line the pita breads with the salad greens and spoon some of the yogurt on top. Serve with the kabobs.

VARIATION

Save time by shaping the meat mixture into burgers. Chill for at least 20 minutes, then broil, basting with the oil and lemon mixture for 15 minutes, turning once. Serve on hamburger buns topped with a little applesauce.

Meat

Steak & Kidney Kabobs

A traditional English dish is transformed for the barbecue.
Marinate the meat overnight if possible to enable the flavors to be fully absorbed.

Makes 4

INGREDIENTS

12 ounces lean steak
2 lamb's kidneys
1 small onion, sliced
$1/2$ tsp dried rosemary

$2/3$ cup dark beer
8 button mushrooms
8 bay leaves
4 tbsp sunflower oil

TO SERVE:
cooked rice
cherry tomatoes

1 Using a sharp knife, trim the steak and cut it into even-size pieces.

2 Cut the kidneys in half and remove the skin. Snip out the core and cut each kidney half into half again.

3 Place the steak and kidney pieces in a shallow, nonmetallic dish.

4 Add the onions and rosemary to the dish and pour the beer over. Cover and marinate in the refrigerator for at least 4 hours or preferably overnight.

5 Remove the meat from the marinade, reserving 4 tbsp of the marinade for basting.

6 Thread the steak and kidney pieces onto the skewers, alternating with the mushrooms and the bay leaves.

7 Stir the oil into the reserved marinade.

8 Broil the kabobs over hot coals for 8–10 minutes, turning and basting with the reserved marinade. Take care not to overcook the kidneys or they will become tough.

9 Serve the kabobs on a bed of cooked rice and with a few cherry tomatoes.

COOK'S TIP

To save time, prepare and marinate the kabobs a day in advance. Place them in a shallow dish and add the marinade. Turn the kabobs occasionally to make sure that they are completely coated in the marinade.

Mixed Broil Skewers

If you like a mixed broil, this dish is for you. The addition of barbecued tomatoes and mushrooms makes this a complete meal.

Serves 4

INGREDIENTS

8 ounces lamb fillet
4 lamb's kidneys
4 thick sausages
8 slices bacon

BASTE:
4 tbsp olive oil
2 tbsp lemon juice
1 tbsp fresh mixed herbs, chopped

TO SERVE:
4 flat mushrooms
2 beefsteak tomatoes

1 Cut the lamb fillet into even-size pieces. Skin and core the kidneys and cut each kidney into 4 pieces.

2 Twist the sausages in the center and cut each sausage in half.

3 Stretch out the bacon slices with the back of a knife.

4 Either wrap the bacon around the sausages or simply roll up the slices on their own. Thread the lamb, sausage, bacon, and kidneys onto skewers.

5 To make the baste, mix together the oil, lemon juice, and mixed herbs in a small bowl until well combined and let stand until required.

6 Broil the kabobs over hot coals, turning and basting frequently, for 8–10 minutes.

7 Cut the tomatoes and mushrooms into large chunks and thread them onto separate skewers. Broil the tomato and mushroom skewers next to the meat for 5 minutes, turning and basting frequently.

8 Transfer the meat skewers to serving plates and serve hot with the tomato and mushroom skewers.

COOK'S TIP

All the elements of this dish can be cooked directly on the barbecue. However, threading them onto skewers makes them quicker and less effort to turn and baste.

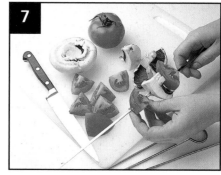

Liver & Onion Kabobs

Liver is full of iron, making this dish nutritious as well as flavorsome.

Makes 4

INGREDIENTS

12 ounces lamb's liver
2 tbsp seasoned all-purpose flour
1/2 tsp dried mixed herbs
4 1/2 ounces bacon

2 medium onions
6 tbsp butter
2 tsp balsamic vinegar

TO SERVE:
mixed salad greens
tomato quarters

---

1 Cut the liver into bite-size pieces. Mix the flour with the dried herbs and toss the liver in the seasoned flour.

2 Stretch out the bacon slices with the back of a knife. Cut each slice in half and wrap the bacon around half of the liver pieces.

3 Thread the plain liver pieces onto skewers, alternating with the bacon-wrapped liver pieces.

4 Cut the onions into rings and thread over the kabobs. Finely chop the onion rings that are too small to thread over the kabobs.

5 Heat the butter in a small pan and sauté the chopped onions for about 5 minutes, until softened. Stir in the vinegar.

6 Brush the butter mixture over the kabobs and broil over hot coals for 8–10 minutes, basting occasionally with the butter mixture, until the liver is just cooked, but is still a little pink inside.

7 Transfer the kabobs to serving plates. Serve with mixed salad greens and tomatoes.

COOK'S TIP

Choose thick slices of liver to give good-sized pieces. Use bacon to hold 2–3 pieces of thinner liver together if necessary.

Vegetables & Salads

You will find all the barbecue extras you will need in this chapter, from extra nibbles and stylish starters to vegetarian main courses and colorful side dishes.

Vegetarians need never feel left out, as many vegetables cook well on the barbecue, and they taste delicious. Try the Colorful Vegetable Kabobs, the Nutty Rice Burgers, the Vegetarian Sausages, or the delicious Marinated Bean Curd Kabobs. Cook vegetables whole, sliced on skewers, or in packets for main dishes or as tasty side dishes.

Keep your diners happy while they wait for the main course with some tasty nibbles, such as Crispy Potato Skins, Garlic Bread, or Mediterranean Bruschetta, while Stuffed Mushrooms and Stuffed Tomatoes make ideal starters for your vegetarian guests.

If you need inspiration for salads to accompany your barbecued food, look no further. All the salads in this chapter go well with barbecued dishes, and many make ideal starters. Pear & Roquefort Salad and Artichoke & Prosciutto Salad are stylish starters that can be prepared well in advance.

Marinated Bean Curd Skewers

Bean curd is full of protein, vitamins, and minerals, and although it is rather bland on its own, it develops a fabulous flavor when it is marinated in garlic and herbs.

Serves 4

INGREDIENTS

12 ounces bean curd
1 red bell pepper
1 yellow bell pepper
2 zucchini
8 button mushrooms

slices of lemon, to garnish

MARINADE:
grated rind and juice of $1/2$ lemon
1 clove garlic, crushed

$1/2$ tsp fresh rosemary, chopped
$1/2$ tsp chopped, fresh thyme
1 tbsp walnut oil

1 To make the marinade, combine the lemon rind and juice, garlic, rosemary, thyme, and oil in a shallow dish.

2 Drain the bean curd, pat it dry on paper towels, and cut it into squares. Add to the marinade and toss to coat. Marinate for 20–30 minutes.

3 Meanwhile, seed and cut the bell peppers into 1-inch pieces. Blanch in boiling water for 4 minutes, rinse in cold water, and drain.

4 Using a canelle knife or potato peeler, remove strips of peel from the zucchini. Cut the zucchini into 1-inch chunks.

5 Remove the bean curd from the marinade, reserving the liquid for basting. Thread the bean curd onto 8 skewers, alternating with the bell pepper pieces, zucchini chunks, and button mushrooms.

6 Broil the skewers over medium hot coals for about 6 minutes, turning and basting

frequently with the reserved marinade.

7 Transfer the skewers to warm serving plates, garnish with slices of lemon, and serve.

VARIATION

For a spicy kabob, make a marinade by mixing together 1 tablespoon of curry paste, 2 tablespoons of oil and the juice of $1/2$ lemon.

Crispy Potato Skins

Use the potato flesh in this recipe for another meal, so make slightly more than you think you need. They make a delicious and tempting starter.

Serves 4–6

INGREDIENTS

8 small baking potatoes, scrubbed
4 tbsp butter, melted
salt and pepper

OPTIONAL TOPPING:
6 scallions, sliced
1/2 cup grated Swiss cheese

1 3/4 ounces salami, cut into
thin strips

1 Preheat the oven to 400°F. Prick the potatoes with a fork and bake for 1 hour, or until tender. Alternatively, cook in a microwave on High for 12–15 minutes.

2 Cut the potatoes in half and scoop out the flesh, leaving about 1/4 inch potato flesh lining the skin.

3 Brush the insides of the potato with melted butter.

4 Place the skins, cut side down, over medium hot coals and broil for 10–15 minutes. Turn the potato skins over and broil for a further 5 minutes or until they are crispy. Take care that they do not burn.

5 Season the potato skins with salt and pepper to taste, transfer to serving plates and serve while they are still warm.

6 The skins can be filled with a variety of different toppings. Broil the potato skins as above for about 10 minutes, then turn cut side up and sprinkle with slices of scallion, grated cheese, and chopped salami. Broil for a further 5 minutes until the cheese just begins to melt. Serve the crispy potato skins hot.

COOK'S TIP

Potato skins can be served on their own, but they are delicious served with a dip. Try a spicy tomato or hummus dip.

Spicy Sweet Potato Slices

Serve these as an accompaniment to other barbecue dishes or with a spicy dip as nibbles. They are ideal at parties if you need to keep guests happy while the main dishes are being cooked.

Serves 4

INGREDIENTS

1 pound sweet potatoes	1 tsp chili sauce	salt and pepper
2 tbsp sunflower oil		

1 Bring a large pan of water to a boil, add the sweet potatoes, and parboil them for 10 minutes. Drain the sweet potatoes thoroughly and transfer to a chopping board.

2 Peel the potatoes and cut them into thick slices.

3 Mix together the oil, chili sauce, and salt and pepper to taste in a small bowl.

4 Brush the spicy mixture liberally over one side of the potatoes. Place the potatoes, oil side down, over medium hot coals and broil for 5–6 minutes.

5 Lightly brush the tops of the potatoes with the oil, turn them over, and broil for a further 5 minutes, or until crisp and golden.

6 Transfer the potatoes to a warm serving dish and serve at once.

COOK'S TIP

Although it is a vegetable, the sweet potato is used in both sweet and savory dishes. It is very versatile and can be boiled, roasted, fried, or cooked, as here, over a barbecue.

VARIATION

For a simple spicy dip combine ⅔ cup sour cream with ½ teaspoon of sugar, ½ teaspoon of Dijon mustard, and salt and pepper to taste. Chill until required.

Barbecued Garlic Potato Wedges

Serve this tasty potato dish with broiled meat or fish.

Serves 4

INGREDIENTS

3 large baking potatoes, scrubbed
4 tbsp olive oil
2 tbsp butter

2 garlic cloves, chopped
1 tbsp chopped, fresh rosemary
1 tbsp chopped, fresh parsley

1 tbsp chopped, fresh thyme
salt and pepper

1 Bring a large pan of water to a boil, add the potatoes, and parboil them for 10 minutes. Drain the potatoes, rinse under cold water, and drain them again thoroughly.

2 Transfer the potatoes to a chopping board. When the potatoes are cold enough to handle, cut them into thick wedges, but do not remove the skins.

3 Heat the oil and butter in a small pan, together with the garlic. Cook gently until the garlic begins to brown, then remove the pan from the heat.

4 Stir the herbs and salt and pepper to taste into the mixture in the pan.

5 Brush the herb mixture all over the potatoes.

6 Broil the potatoes over hot coals for 10–15 minutes, brushing liberally with any of the remaining herb and butter mixture, or until the potatoes are just tender.

7 Transfer the barbecued garlic potatoes to a warm serving plate and serve as a starter or as a side dish.

COOK'S TIP

You may find it easier to barbecue these potatoes in a hinged rack or in a specially designed barbecue roasting tray.

Vegetarian Sausages

The deliciously cheesy flavor is certain to make these sausages a hit with vegetarians who have no need to feel left out when it comes to tasty barbecued food.

Makes 8

INGREDIENTS

1 tbsp sunflower oil
1 small onion, finely chopped
3/4 cup finely chopped mushrooms
1/2 red bell pepper, seeded and
  finely chopped

14 ounce can cannolini beans, rinsed
  and drained
1 2/3 cups fresh breadcrumbs
1 cup grated cheddar cheese
1 tsp dried mixed herbs
1 egg yolk

seasoned all-purpose flour
oil, to baste

TO SERVE:
rolls
slices of fried onion

1 Heat the oil in a saucepan and sauté the prepared onion, mushrooms, and bell peppers until softened.

2 Mash the cannolini beans in a large mixing bowl. Add the onion, mushroom, and bell pepper mixture, the breadcrumbs, cheese, herbs, and egg yolk, and mix together well.

3 Press the mixture together with your fingers and shape into 8 sausages.

4 Roll each sausage in the seasoned flour to coat well. Chill in the refrigerator for at least 30 minutes.

5 Broil the sausages on a sheet of oiled foil set over medium coals for 15–20 minutes, turning and basting frequently with oil, until golden.

6 Split a roll down the middle and insert a layer of fried onions. Place the sausage in the roll and serve.

COOK'S TIP

Take care not to break the sausages when you are turning them over. If you have a hinged rack, oil this and place the sausages inside, turning and oiling frequently. Look for racks that are especially designed for barbecuing sausages.

Nutty Rice Burgers

Serve these burgers in toasted sesame seed buns. If you wish, add a slice of cheese to top the burger at the end of cooking.

Makes 6

INGREDIENTS

1 tbsp sunflower oil
1 small onion, finely chopped
1 1/2 cups finely chopped mushrooms
8 cups cooked brown rice
1 2/3 cups breadcrumbs
3/4 cup walnuts, chopped
1 egg

2 tbsp brown fruity sauce
dash of Tabasco sauce
salt and pepper
oil, to baste
6 individual cheese slices (optional)

TO SERVE:
6 sesame seed buns
slices of onion
slices of tomato
salad greens

1 Heat the oil in a large saucepan and sauté the onions for 3–4 minutes, until they just begin to soften. Add the mushrooms and cook for a further 2 minutes.

2 Remove the pan from the heat and mix the rice, breadcrumbs, walnuts, egg, and sauces into the vegetables. Season with salt and pepper and mix well.

3 Shape the mixture into 6 burgers, pressing the mixture together with your fingers. Chill in the refrigerator for at least 30 minutes.

4 Broil the burgers on an oiled rack over medium coals for 5–6 minutes on each side, turning once and frequently basting with oil.

5 If desired, top the burgers with a slice of cheese 2 minutes before the end of the cooking time. Broil the onion and tomato slices.

6 Toast the sesame seed rolls at the side of the barbecue. Serve the burgers in the rolls, together with the barbecued onions and tomatoes.

COOK'S TIP

It is quicker and more economical to use leftover rice to make these burgers. However, if you are cooking the rice for this dish you will need to use 1 cup uncooked long grain rice.

Eggplant & Mozzarella Sandwiches

Serve these sandwiches as a vegetarian main course for two or as a side dish to accompany other barbecued foods.

Serves 2

INGREDIENTS

1 large eggplant	1 cup grated mozzarella cheese	TO SERVE:
1 tbsp lemon juice	2 sun-dried tomatoes, chopped	Italian bread
3 tbsp olive oil	salt and pepper	mixed salad greens
		slices of tomato

1 Slice the eggplant into thin rounds.

2 Mix the lemon juice and olive oil in a small bowl until well combined and season the mixture with salt and pepper to taste.

3 Brush the eggplant slices with the oil and lemon juice mixture and broil over medium hot coals for 2–3 minutes, without turning, until they are golden on the underside.

4 Turn half of the eggplant slices over and sprinkle with cheese and chopped sun-dried tomatoes.

5 Place the remaining eggplant slices on top of the cheese and tomatoes, turning them so that the pale side is uppermost.

6 Broil for 1–2 minutes, then carefully turn the whole sandwich over, and broil for 1–2 minutes. Baste with the oil mixture.

7 Serve with Italian bread, mixed salad greens, and a few slices of tomato.

VARIATION

Try feta cheese instead of mozzarella but omit the salt from the basting oil because feta is quite salty. A creamy goat's cheese would be equally delicious.

Charbroiled Eggplant

The wonderful flavor and texture of charbroiled eggplant is hard to beat.
Serve plain as a simple vegetable dish, but for a tasty starter or vegetarian dish,
serve it accompanied with pesto or minty cucumber sauce.

Serves 4

INGREDIENTS

1 large eggplant
3 tbsp olive oil
1 tsp sesame oil
salt and pepper

PESTO:
1 clove garlic
$^1/_4$ cup pine nuts
$^1/_4$ cup fresh basil leaves
2 tbsp Parmesan cheese
6 tbsp olive oil
salt and pepper

CUCUMBER SAUCE:
$^2/_3$ cup unsweetened yogurt
2-inch piece cucumber
$^1/_2$ tsp mint sauce

1 Remove the stalk from the eggplant, then cut it lengthwise into 8 thin slices.

2 Lay the slices on a plate or board and sprinkle them liberally with salt to remove the bitter juices. Set aside.

3 Meanwhile, prepare the baste. Combine the olive and sesame oils, season with pepper, and set aside.

4 To make the pesto, put the garlic, pine nuts, basil, and cheese in a food processor until finely chopped. With the machine running, gradually add the oil in a thin stream. Season to taste.

5 To make the minty cucumber sauce, place the yogurt in a mixing bowl. Remove the seeds from the cucumber and dice the flesh finely. Stir into the yogurt with the mint sauce.

6 Rinse the eggplant slices and pat them dry on absorbent paper towels. Baste with the oil mixture and broil over hot coals for about 10 minutes, turning once. The eggplant should be golden and tender.

7 Transfer the eggplant slices to warm individual serving plates and serve immediately with either the cucumber sauce or the pesto.

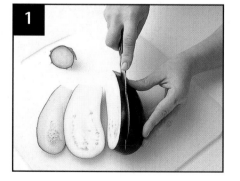

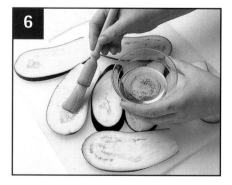

Stuffed Tomatoes

These barbecued tomato cups are filled with a delicious
Greek-style combination of herbs, nuts, and raisins.

Makes 8

INGREDIENTS

4 beefsteak tomatoes	3 tbsp chopped, fresh mint	3 tbsp raisins
4^1/2 cups cooked rice	2 tbsp chopped, fresh parsley	2 tsp olive oil
8 scallions, chopped	3 tbsp pine nuts	salt and pepper

1 Cut the tomatoes in half, then scoop out the seeds, and discard.

2 Stand the tomatoes upside down on absorbent paper towels for a few moments in order to allow all of the juices to drain out.

3 Turn the tomatoes upright and sprinkle the insides with salt and pepper.

4 Mix together the rice, scallions, mint, parsley, pine nuts, and raisins. Spoon the mixture into the tomato cups.

5 Drizzle a little olive oil over the tomatoes, then broil them on an oiled rack over medium hot coals for about 10 minutes until they are tender.

6 Transfer the tomatoes to warm serving plates and serve immediately.

VARIATION

Cook regular tomatoes, cut in half, brushed with oil, and seasoned with salt and pepper, broiling them cut side down first.

COOK'S TIP

Tomatoes are a popular barbecue vegetable and can be quickly cooked. Try broiling slices of beefsteak tomato and slices of onion brushed with a little oil and topped with sprigs of fresh herbs. In addition, cherry tomatoes can be threaded onto skewers and broiled for 5–10 minutes until hot.

Colorful Vegetable Kabobs

Brighten up a barbecue meal with these colorful kabobs.
They are basted with a flavored oil.

Serves 4

INGREDIENTS

1 red bell pepper, seeded
1 yellow bell pepper, seeded
1 green bell pepper, seeded
1 small onion

8 cherry tomatoes
3¹/₂ ounces mushrooms

SEASONED OIL:
6 tbsp olive oil
1 clove garlic, crushed
¹/₂ tsp mixed dried herbs or herbes de Provence

1 Cut the bell peppers into 1-inch pieces.

2 Peel the onion and cut it into wedges, leaving the root end just intact to help keep the wedges together.

3 Thread the bell peppers, onion wedges, tomatoes, and mushrooms onto skewers, alternating the colors of the bell peppers.

4 To make the seasoned oil, mix together the oil, garlic, and herbs in a small bowl until well combined. Brush the mixture liberally over the kabobs until well coated.

5 Broil the kabobs over medium hot coals for 10–15 minutes, brushing the vegetables with more of the seasoned oil and turning the skewers frequently.

6 Transfer the vegetable kabobs to warm individual serving plates. Serve with walnut sauce (see Cook's Tip), if you wish.

COOK'S TIP

These kabobs are delicious when accompanied with a walnut sauce. To make the sauce, process 1 cup walnuts in a food processor until they form a smooth paste. With the machine running, add ²/₃ cup heavy cream and 1 tablespoon of olive oil. Season to taste. Alternatively, finely chop the walnuts, then pound them in a mortar with a pestle to form a paste. Mix with the cream and oil, and season.

Charbroiled Mixed Vegetables

This combination of barbecued vegetables is a perfect
accompaniment for barbecued meat or fish.

Serves 4–6

INGREDIENTS

8 baby eggplant
4 zucchini
2 red onions
4 tomatoes
salt and pepper

1 tsp balsamic vinegar, to serve

BASTE:
6 tbsp butter
2 tsp walnut oil

2 cloves garlic, chopped
4 tbsp dry white wine or cider

1 To prepare the vegetables, cut the eggplant in half. Trim and cut the zucchini in half lengthwise. Thickly slice the onion and halve the tomatoes.

2 Season all of the vegetables with salt and black pepper to taste.

3 To make the baste, melt the butter with the oil in a saucepan. Add the garlic and cook gently for 1–2 minutes. Remove the pan from the heat and stir in the wine or cider.

4 Add the vegetables to the pan and toss them in the baste mixture. You may need to do this in several batches to ensure that all of the vegetables are coated evenly with the baste mixture.

5 Remove the vegetables from the baste mixture, reserving any excess baste. Place the vegetables on an oiled rack over medium hot coals. Broil for 15–20 minutes, basting with the reserved baste mixture and turning once or twice during cooking.

6 Transfer the vegetables to warm serving plates and serve sprinkled with balsamic vinegar.

COOK'S TIP

Use a long-handled brush for basting food on the barbecue.

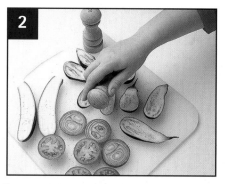

Stuffed Mushrooms

Serve these mushrooms as a side vegetable or as an appetizer. For non-vegetarians, replace the cheese with chopped chorizo sausage.

Makes 12

INGREDIENTS

12 open-cap mushrooms
4 scallions, chopped
4 tsp olive oil

2 cups fresh brown breadcrumbs
1 tsp fresh oregano, chopped

$3^1/2$ ounces feta cheese or
chorizo sausage

1 Remove the stalks from the mushrooms and chop the stalks finely.

2 Sauté the mushroom stalks and scallions in half of the oil.

3 Transfer the mushroom stalks and scallions to a large mixing bowl. Add the breadcrumbs and oregano to the mushrooms and scallions, mix, and set aside until required.

4 If using feta, crumble the cheese into small pieces in a small bowl, using a fork or your fingers.

5 If you are using chorizo sausage, remove the skin and chop the flesh finely.

6 Add the cheese or chorizo to the breadcrumb mixture and mix well.

7 Spoon the stuffing mixture into the mushroom caps.

8 Drizzle the oil over the mushrooms. Broil on an oiled rack over medium hot coals for 8–10 minutes.

9 Transfer the mushrooms to serving plates and serve hot.

COOK'S TIP

If only small mushrooms are available, place a sheet of oiled foil on top of the barbecue rack and cook the mushrooms on this. This will stop the smaller mushrooms from cooking too quickly and burning, and it will also prevent any excess stuffing mixture from dropping onto the coals during cooking.

Corn Cobs

There are a number of ways of cooking corn cobs on the barbecue.
Leaving on the husks protects the tender corn niblets.

Serves 4

INGREDIENTS

4 corn cobs, with husks	1 tsp chopped, fresh chives	salt and pepper
8 tbsp butter	1 tsp chopped, fresh thyme	
1 tbsp chopped, fresh parsley	rind of 1 lemon, grated	

1 To prepare the corn cobs, peel back the husks and remove the silken hairs.

2 Fold back the husks and secure them in place with string if necessary.

3 Blanch the corn cobs in a large saucepan of boiling water for about 5 minutes, in batches if necessary. Remove the cobs with a slotted spoon and drain thoroughly.

4 Broil the cobs over medium hot coals for 20–30 minutes, turning frequently.

5 Meanwhile, soften the butter and beat in the parsley, chives, thyme, lemon rind, and salt and pepper to taste.

6 Transfer the corn cobs to serving plates, remove the string and pull back the husks. Serve with a generous portion of herb butter.

COOK'S TIP

Cooking the cobs with the husk still on allows them to retain more moisture during barbecuing, so they won't dry out.

COOK'S TIP

When you are buying fresh corn, look for plump, tightly packed kernels. If you are unable to get fresh cobs, cook frozen corn cobs on the barbecue. Spread some of the herb butter onto a sheet of double thickness foil. Wrap the cobs in the foil and broil among the coals for about 20–30 minutes.

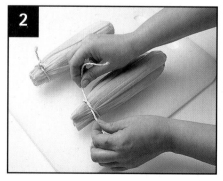

Pumpkin Packets with Chili & Lime

This spicy side dish is perfect for a Halloween barbecue.

Serves 4

INGREDIENTS

1 pound 9 ounces pumpkin or squash
2 tbsp sunflower oil

2 tbsp butter
1/2 tsp chili sauce

rind of 1 lime, grated
2 tsp lime juice

1 Halve the pumpkin or squash and scoop out the seeds. Rinse the seeds and reserve. Cut the pumpkin into thin wedges and peel.

2 Heat the oil and butter together in a large saucepan, stirring continuously until melted. Stir in the chili sauce, lime rind, and juice.

3 Add the pumpkin or squash and seeds to the pan and toss to coat on all sides in the flavored butter.

4 Divide the mixture among 4 double-thickness sheets of foil. Fold the foil to enclose the pumpkin or squash mixture completely.

5 Cook the foil packets over hot coals for 15–25 minutes, or until the pumpkin or squash is cooked through and tender.

6 Transfer the foil packets to warm serving plates. Open the packets at the table and serve at once.

VARIATION

Add 2 teaspoons of curry paste to the oil instead of the lime and chili. Use butternut squash when pumpkin is not available.

COOK'S TIP

Always take care when you handle chilies. It is a good idea to wear disposable gloves when you are slicing and seeding them. Alternatively, rub a little oil over your fingers before you begin—the oil will help to prevent your skin from absorbing the chili juice. Wash your hands thoroughly afterward.

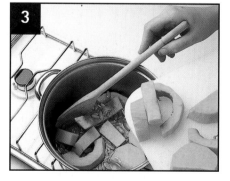

Garlic Bread

A perennial favorite, garlic bread is perfect with a range of barbecue meals.

Serves 6

INGREDIENTS

³/₄ cup butter, softened
3 cloves garlic, crushed

2 tbsp chopped, fresh parsley
pepper

1 large or 2 small loaves of
French bread

1 Mix together the butter, garlic, and parsley in a bowl until well combined. Season to taste with pepper and mix well.

2 Cut the French bread into thick slices.

3 Spread the flavored butter over one side of each slice and reassemble the loaf on a large sheet of thick foil.

4 Wrap the bread well and cook over hot coals for 10–15 minutes, until the butter melts and the bread is piping hot.

5 Serve as an accompaniment to a wide range of dishes.

VARIATION

For a tasty variation, sprinkle a little grated mozzarella cheese between each slice of bread. Reassemble the loaf and cook for 10–15 minutes, until the cheese has just melted.

COOK'S TIP

Some recipes suggest that you do not cut all the way through the bread when you slice it, but you will find it a lot easier to serve if you do. Simply keep the slices in order and reassemble once buttered.

COOK'S TIP

When garlic is cooked like this on a barbecue, the sweetness of it comes to the fore. Garlic combines well with fresh, crusty white bread and the result tastes delicious.

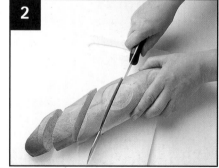

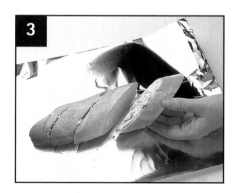

Mediterranean Bruschetta

This modern version of garlic bread originates from Italy. It is important to use a good quality olive oil for this recipe. Serve the bruschetta with kabobs or fish for a really summery taste.

Serves 4

INGREDIENTS

1 Italian loaf or small loaf of French bread

1 plump clove garlic
extra virgin olive oil

freshly grated Parmesan cheese, (optional)

1 Slice the bread in half crosswise and again lengthwise to give 4 portions.

2 Do not peel the garlic clove, but cut it in half using a sharp knife.

3 Broil the bread over hot coals for a few minutes on both sides until golden brown.

4 Rub the garlic, cut side down, all over the toasted surface of the bread.

5 Drizzle the olive oil over the bread and serve hot as an accompaniment.

6 If using Parmesan cheese, sprinkle the cheese over the bread. Return the bread to the barbecue, cut side up, for 1–2 minutes, until the cheese just begins to melt. Serve hot.

COOK'S TIP

As ready-grated Parmesan quickly loses its pungency and "bite," it is better to buy small quantities of the cheese in one piece and grate it yourself as needed. Tightly wrapped in plastic wrap or foil, it will keep in the refrigerator for several months. Grate it just before using, for maximum flavor.

VARIATION

For a tasty appetizer, serve the bruschetta topped with chopped tomatoes mixed with a few chopped anchovies or olives.

COOK'S TIP

If you do not peel the garlic, the smell will not transfer to your fingers.

Caesar Salad

This traditional—now world-famous—salad has a good robust flavor.

Serves 6-8

INGREDIENTS

2 thick slices of white bread	1 clove garlic	DRESSING:
2 tbsp sunflower oil	1 3/4 ounces Parmesan cheese	1 small egg
2 slices fatty bacon	1 large romaine lettuce	juice 1 lemon
		6 tbsp olive oil
		salt and white pepper

1 To make the croûtons, remove the crusts from the bread and discard. Cut the bread into small cubes. Heat the oil in a skillet and fry the bread cubes until golden brown. Drain the bread cubes thoroughly on absorbent paper towels.

2 Chop the bacon and fry until crisp. Drain on absorbent paper towels.

3 Cut the garlic in half and rub all around the inside of a serving dish. This will give the salad just a hint of garlic.

4 Wash the lettuce, tear into bite-size pieces, and place in the serving dish.

5 Using a vegetable peeler, shave peelings off the cheese.

6 To make the dressing, whisk the egg in a small bowl. Gradually whisk in the lemon juice and oil. Season with salt and pepper to taste.

7 Pour the salad dressing over the lettuce and toss to coat. Serve sprinkled with the croûtons, bacon, and Parmesan shavings.

COOK'S TIP

Pregnant women, children, and people with weak immune systems may wish to avoid eating recipes containing raw egg.

VARIATION

Use 6 chopped anchovies instead of the bacon, if you prefer.

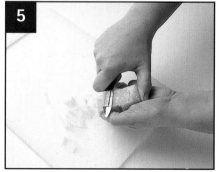

Coleslaw

*Always popular, homemade coleslaw tastes far
superior to any that you can buy.*

Serves 10-12

INGREDIENTS

²/₃ cup mayonnaise

²/₃ cup low-fat unsweetened yogurt

dash of Tabasco sauce

1 medium head white cabbage

4 carrots

1 green bell pepper

2 tbsp sunflower seeds

salt and pepper

1 To make the dressing, combine the mayonnaise, yogurt, Tabasco sauce, and salt and pepper to taste in a small bowl. Leave to chill in the refrigerator until required.

2 Cut the cabbage in half and then into quarters. Remove and discard the tough center stalk. Shred the cabbage leaves finely. Wash the leaves and dry them thoroughly.

3 Peel the carrot and shred in a food processor. Alternatively, coarsely grate the carrot.

4 Quarter and seed the bell pepper and cut the flesh into thin strips.

5 Combine the vegetables in a large serving bowl and toss to mix. Pour the dressing on and toss until the vegetables are well coated. Let chill.

6 Just before serving, place the sunflower seeds on a cookie sheet and toast them in the oven or under the broiler until golden brown.

7 Scatter the sesame seeds over the coleslaw and serve.

COOK'S TIP

You can make coleslaw a few days in advance. To ensure that the sunflower seeds are crispy, add them just before serving.

VARIATION

For a slightly different taste, add one or more of the following ingredients to the coleslaw: raisins, grapes, grated apple, chopped walnuts, cubes of cheese, or roasted peanuts.

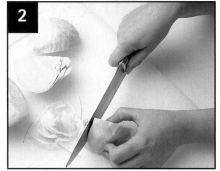

Green Bean & Carrot Salad

*This colorful salad of crisp vegetables is
tossed in a delicious sun-dried tomato dressing.*

Serves 4

INGREDIENTS

12 ounces green beans	DRESSING:	1/4 tsp superfine sugar
8 ounces carrots	2 tbsp extra virgin olive oil	salt and pepper
1 red bell pepper	1 tbsp red wine vinegar	
1 red onion	2 tsp sun-dried tomato paste	

1 Top and tail the beans and blanch them in boiling water for 4 minutes, until just tender. Drain the beans and rinse them under cold water until they are cool. Drain the beans again thoroughly.

2 Transfer the beans to a large salad bowl.

3 Peel the carrots and cut them into thin matchsticks.

4 Halve and seed the bell pepper and cut the flesh into thin strips.

5 Peel the onion and cut it into thin slices.

6 Add the carrot, bell pepper, and onion to the beans and toss to mix.

7 To make the dressing, place the oil, wine vinegar, sun-dried tomato paste, sugar, and salt and pepper to taste in a small screw-top jar and shake well.

8 Pour the dressing over the vegetables and serve immediately or chill in the refrigerator until required.

COOK'S TIP

*Use canned beans if fresh ones are
unavailable. Rinse off the salty
liquid and drain well. There is no
need to blanch canned beans.*

Spinach & Orange Salad

This is a refreshing and very nutritious salad. Add the dressing just before serving so that the leaves do not become soggy.

Serves 4–6

INGREDIENTS

8 ounces young spinach leaves
2 large oranges
$^1/_2$ red onion

DRESSING:
3 tbsp extra virgin olive oil
2 tbsp freshly squeezed orange juice
2 tsp lemon juice

1 tsp clear honey
$^1/_2$ tsp wholegrain mustard
salt and pepper

1 Wash the spinach leaves under cold running water and then dry them thoroughly on absorbent paper towels. Remove any tough stalks and tear the larger leaves into smaller pieces.

2 Slice the top and bottom off each orange with a sharp knife, then remove the peel.

3 Carefully slice between the membranes of the orange to remove the segments.

4 Using a sharp knife, finely chop the onion.

5 Mix together the spinach leaves and orange segments and arrange in a serving dish.

6 Scatter the chopped onion over the salad.

7 To make the dressing, whisk together the olive oil, orange juice, lemon juice, honey, mustard, and salt and pepper to taste in a small bowl.

8 Pour the dressing over the salad just before serving. Toss the salad well to coat the leaves with the dressing.

COOK'S TIP

Tear the spinach leaves into bite-size pieces rather than cutting them because cutting bruises the leaves.

VARIATION

Use a mixture of spinach and watercress leaves, if you prefer a slightly more peppery flavor.

Potato Salad

You can use leftover cold potatoes, cut into bite-size pieces, for this salad. If you are making it from scratch, use tiny new potatoes for maximum flavor.

Serves 4

INGREDIENTS

1 pound 9 ounces tiny new potatoes
8 scallions
1 hard-cooked egg (optional)
generous 1 cup mayonnaise

1 tsp paprika
salt and pepper

TO GARNISH:
2 tbsp snipped chives
pinch of paprika

1 Bring a large pan of lightly salted water to a boil. Add the potatoes to the pan and cook for 10–15 minutes, or until they are just tender.

2 Drain the potatoes in a colander and rinse them under cold running water until they are completely cold. Drain them again thoroughly. Transfer the potatoes to a mixing bowl and set aside until required.

3 Using a sharp knife, trim and slice the scallions thinly on the diagonal.

4 Shell and chop the hard-cooked egg, if using.

5 Combine the mayonnaise, paprika, and salt and pepper to taste in a bowl. Pour the mixture over the potatoes.

6 Add the scallions and egg (if using) to the potatoes and toss together.

7 Transfer the potato salad to a serving bowl, sprinkle with snipped chives and a pinch of paprika. Cover and chill in the refrigerator until required.

VARIATION

To make a lighter dressing, use a mixture of half mayonnaise and half unsweetened yogurt.

VARIATION

Add cubes of cheese to the potato salad, if liked.

Tabouleh

*The fresh crunchy texture of this popular Middle Eastern
dish is perfect with barbecued foods.*

Serves 4

INGREDIENTS

1^1/$_2$ cups cracked wheat
8 ounces tomatoes
1 small onion
^{1}/$_4$ cucumber

^{1}/$_2$ red bell pepper
4 tbsp chopped, fresh parsley
3 tbsp chopped, fresh mint
2 tbsp pine nuts

4 tbsp lemon juice
4 tbsp extra virgin olive oil
2 cloves garlic, crushed
salt and pepper

1 Place the cracked wheat in a large bowl and cover with plenty of boiling water. Let stand for about 30 minutes, or until the grains are tender and have swelled in size.

2 Drain the wheat through a large strainer. Press down with a plate in order to remove as much water as possible. Transfer the wheat to a large mixing bowl.

3 Cut the tomatoes in half, scoop out the seeds, and discard them. Chop the flesh into fine dice.

4 Using a sharp knife, finely chop the onion.

5 Scoop out the seeds from the cucumber and discard them. Finely dice the cucumber flesh.

6 Seed the bell peppers and chop the flesh.

7 Add the prepared vegetables to the wheat, with the herbs and pine nuts. Toss until mixed.

8 Mix together the lemon juice oil, garlic, and salt and pepper to taste in a small bowl.

9 Pour the mixture over the wheat and vegetables and toss together. Chill in the refrigerator until required.

COOK'S TIP

This salad is best made a few hours before it is required to allow time for the flavors to develop and blend together. It can even be made a few days ahead, if wished.

Hot Lentil Salad with Balsamic Dressing

A robust vinaigrette dressing is served with this warm salad.
If you prefer, you can serve the salad cold.

Serves 6–8

INGREDIENTS

$^3/_4$ cup Puy lentils, cooked
4 tbsp olive oil
1 small onion, sliced
4 stalks celery, sliced
2 cloves garlic, crushed

2 zucchini, trimmed and diced
$4^1/_2$ ounces green beans, trimmed
   and cut into short lengths
$^1/_2$ red bell pepper, seeded and diced
$^1/_2$ yellow bell pepper, seeded
   and diced

1 tsp Dijon mustard
1 tbsp balsamic vinegar
salt and pepper

1 Place the lentils in a large mixing or serving bowl. The lentils can still be warm, if wished.

2 Heat the oil in a saucepan and sauté the onion and celery for 2–3 minutes, until softened but not browned.

3 Add the garlic, zucchini, and green beans to the pan and cook for a further 2 minutes, stirring occasionally.

4 Add the bell peppers to the pan and cook for 1 minute.

5 Stir the mustard and the balsamic vinegar into the pan and mix until warm and thoroughly combined.

6 Pour the warm mixture over the lentils and toss together to mix well. Season with salt and pepper to taste and serve immediately.

COOK'S TIP

To cook the lentils, rinse them well and place in a large saucepan. Cover with plenty of cold water and bring to a boil. Boil rapidly for 10 minutes, then reduce the heat, and simmer for 35 minutes, until the lentils are tender. Drain well.

Italian Mozzarella Salad

This colorful salad is packed full of delicious flavors, but is easy to make.

Serves 6

INGREDIENTS

7 ounces young spinach
$4^1/_2$ ounces watercress
$4^1/_2$ ounces mozzarella cheese

8 ounces cherry tomatoes
2 tsp balsamic vinegar
$1^1/_2$ tbsp extra virgin olive oil

salt and freshly ground black pepper

1 Wash the spinach and watercress and drain thoroughly on absorbent paper towels. Remove any tough stalks. Place the spinach and watercress leaves in a serving dish.

2 Cut the mozzarella into small pieces and scatter them over the spinach and watercress leaves.

3 Cut the cherry tomatoes in half and scatter them over the salad.

4 Sprinkle with the balsamic vinegar and oil, and season with salt and pepper to taste. Toss the mixture together to coat the leaves. Serve at once or chill in the refrigerator until required.

COOK'S TIP

Mozzarella is a highly popular cheese. It is a soft, fresh cheese with a piquant flavor, traditionally made from water buffalo's milk. It is usually sold surrounded by whey to keep it moist. Buffalo milk is now scarce, and so nowadays this cheese is often made with cow's milk. Mozzarella combines well with tomatoes, and this combination is now a classic.

VARIATION

Include feta or halloumi cheese instead of mozzarella for a change, and use sherry vinegar instead of balsamic vinegar, if preferred.

Artichoke & Prosciutto Salad

This elegant salad would make a good first course. Serve it with a little fresh bread for mopping up the juices.

Serves 4

INGREDIENTS

9$^1/_2$ ounce can artichoke hearts in oil, drained
4 small tomatoes
$^1/_2$ cup sun-dried tomatoes in oil
1$^1/_2$ ounces prosciutto

$^1/_2$ cup pitted black olives, halved
few basil leaves

DRESSING:
3 tbsp olive oil

1 tbsp white wine vinegar
1 clove garlic, crushed
$^1/_2$ tsp mild mustard
1 tsp clear honey
salt and pepper

1 Make sure the artichoke hearts are thoroughly drained, then cut them into quarters, and place in a bowl.

2 Cut each fresh tomato into wedges. Slice the sun-dried tomatoes into thin strips. Cut the prosciutto into thin strips and add to the bowl with the tomatoes and olive halves.

3 Keeping a few basil leaves whole for garnishing, tear the remainder of the leaves into small pieces and add to the bowl containing the other salad ingredients.

4 To make the dressing, put the oil, wine vinegar, garlic, mustard, honey, and salt and pepper to taste in a screw-top jar and shake vigorously until the ingredients are well blended.

5 Pour the dressing over the salad and toss together.

6 Serve the salad garnished with a few whole basil leaves.

COOK'S TIP

Use bottled artichokes in oil if you can find them, as they have a better flavor. If only canned artichokes are available, rinse them carefully to remove the salty liquid.

Pear & Roquefort Salad

The sweetness of the pear is a perfect partner to the "bite" of the radiccio.

Serves 4

INGREDIENTS

1³/₄ ounces Roquefort cheese
²/₃ cup low-fat unsweetened yogurt
2 tbsp snipped chives

few leaves of lollo rosso
few leaves of radiccio
few leaves of corn salad

2 ripe pears
pepper
whole chives, to garnish

1 Place the cheese in a bowl and mash with a fork. Gradually blend the yogurt into the cheese to make a smooth dressing. Add the chives and season with pepper to taste.

2 Tear the lollo rosso, radiccio, and corn salad leaves into manageable pieces. Arrange the salad greens on a serving platter or on individual serving plates.

3 Quarter and core the pears, and then cut them into slices.

4 Arrange the pear slices over the salad greens.

5 Drizzle the dressing over the pears and garnish with a few whole chives. Serve at once.

COOK'S TIP

Look for bags of mixed salad greens, as these are generally more economical than buying lots of different greens separately. If you are using greens that have not been prewashed, rinse them well and dry them thoroughly on absorbent paper towels or in a salad spinner. Alternatively, wrap the greens in a clean dish cloth and shake dry.

COOK'S TIP

Arrange the Pear & Roquefort Salad on individual plates for an attractive starter, or on one large serving platter for a side salad.

Pasta Salad with Basil Vinaigrette

*All the ingredients of pesto sauce are included in this salad, which
has a fabulous summery taste, perfect for al fresco eating.*

Serves 4

INGREDIENTS

2 cups fusilli (pasta spirals)

4 tomatoes

1/3 cup black olives

1/2 cup sun-dried tomatoes in oil

2 tbsp pine nuts

2 tbsp grated Parmesan cheese
fresh basil, to garnish

VINAIGRETTE:

1/4 cup basil leaves

1 clove garlic

2 tbsp grated Parmesan cheese

4 tbsp extra virgin olive oil

2 tbsp lemon juice

salt and pepper

1 Cook the pasta in lightly salted boiling water for 10–12 minutes, until just tender, or according to the instructions on the packet. Drain the pasta, rinse under cold water, then drain again thoroughly. Place the pasta in a large bowl.

2 To make the vinaigrette, place the basil leaves, garlic, cheese, oil, and lemon juice in a food processor. Season with salt and pepper to taste. Process until the leaves are well chopped and the ingredients are combined.

Alternatively, finely chop the basil leaves by hand and combine with the other vinaigrette ingredients. Pour the vinaigrette over the pasta and toss to coat.

3 Cut the tomatoes into wedges. Pit and halve the olives. Slice the sun-dried tomatoes. Toast the pine nuts on a cookie sheet under the broiler until golden.

4 Add the tomatoes (fresh and sun-dried) and the olives to the pasta and mix until combined.

5 Transfer the pasta to a serving dish, scatter over the Parmesan and pine nuts, and garnish with a few basil leaves.

COOK'S TIP

Sun-dried tomatoes have a strong, intense flavor. They are most frequently found packed in oil with herbs and garlic. Do not waste the oil, which has an excellent flavor, instead use it in salad dressings.

Mango & Wild Rice Salad

Wild rice is, in fact, an aquatic grass that is native to North America. It has a delicious nutty flavor and a slightly chewy texture.

Serves 6

INGREDIENTS

1/2 cup wild rice	3 stalks celery	2 tbsp chopped, fresh cilantro
1 cup Basmati rice	1/4 cup ready-to-eat dried	or mint
3 tbsp hazelnut oil	apricots, chopped	salt and pepper
1 tbsp sherry vinegar	3/4 cup slivered almonds	sprigs of fresh cilantro or mint,
1 ripe mango		to garnish

1 Cook the rice in separate saucepans in lightly salted boiling water. Cook the wild rice for 45–50 minutes, and the Basmati rice for 10–12 minutes. Drain, rinse well, and drain again. Place the rice in a large bowl.

2 Mix the oil, vinegar, and seasoning together. Pour the mixture over the rice and toss well.

3 Cut the mango in half lengthwise, as close to the pit as possible. Remove and discard the pit.

4 Peel the skin from the mango and cut the flesh into slices.

5 Slice the celery thinly and add to the cooled rice with the mango, apricots, almonds, and chopped herbs. Toss together and transfer to a serving dish. Garnish with sprigs of fresh herbs.

COOK'S TIP

Add dressings to rice salads while the rice is still hot because the rice will absorb the flavor better.

COOK'S TIP

To toast almonds, place them on a cookie sheet in a preheated oven at 350°F for 5–10 minutes. Alternatively, toast them under the broiler, turning frequently and keeping a close eye on them because they will quickly burn.

Mixed Bean Salad

Use a mixture of any canned beans in this crunchy, very filling salad.

Serves 6–8

INGREDIENTS

14 ounce can small navy
  beans, drained
14 ounce can red kidney
  beans, drained
14 ounce can dried lima
  beans, drained

1 small red onion, thinly sliced
6 ounces dwarf green beans, topped
  and tailed
1 red bell pepper, halved and seeded

DRESSING:
4 tbsp olive oil
2 tbsp sherry vinegar
2 tbsp lemon juice
1 tsp light muscovado sugar
1 tsp chili sauce (optional)

1 Put the canned beans in a large mixing bowl. Add the sliced onion and mix together.

2 Cut the dwarf green beans in half and cook in lightly salted boiling water for about 8 minutes, until just tender. Rinse under cold water and drain again. Add to the mixed beans and onions.

3 Place the bell pepper halves, cut side down, on a broiler rack and cook until the skin blackens and chars. Cool slightly, then put them into a plastic bag for about 10 minutes. Peel away the skin from the bell peppers and discard. Roughly chop the bell pepper flesh and add it to the beans.

4 To make the dressing, place the oil, sherry vinegar, lemon juice, sugar, and chili sauce (if using) in a screw-top jar and shake vigorously.

5 Pour the dressing over the mixed bean salad and toss well. Chill in the refrigerator until required.

VARIATION

You can use any combination of beans in this salad. For a distinctive flavor, add 1 teaspoon of curry paste instead of the chili sauce.

VARIATION

Add some flaked tuna fish or garlic sausage to turn this side salad into a main meal.

Mediterranean Bell Pepper Salad

*This salad is full of fabulous Mediterranean flavors and it goes well
with all barbecued foods, especially meats. Alternatively, serve it with a selection
of French and Italian breads for a simple starter.*

Serves 4

INGREDIENTS

2 red bell peppers, halved and seeded
2 yellow bell peppers, halved
  and seeded
3 tbsp extra virgin olive oil

1 onion, cut into wedges
2 large zucchini, sliced
2 garlic cloves, sliced
1 tbsp balsamic vinegar
1³/₄ ounces anchovy fillets, chopped

¹/₄ cup pitted black olives, quartered
fresh basil leaves

1 Place the bell pepper halves, cut side down, on a broiler pan and cook until the skin blackens and chars. Cool slightly, then put them into a plastic bag for about 10 minutes.

2 Peel away the skin from the bell peppers and discard. Cut the flesh into thick strips.

3 Heat the oil in a large skillet, add the onion, and sauté gently for 10 minutes, or until softened. Add the zucchini slices, garlic, and bell pepper strips to the skillet and cook, stirring occasionally, for a further 10 minutes.

4 Add the vinegar, anchovies, and olives to the pan. Season to taste. Mix well and let cool.

5 Reserve a few basil leaves for garnishing, then tear the remainder into small pieces. Stir them into the salad.

6 Transfer the salad to a serving dish and garnish with a few whole basil leaves.

COOK'S TIP

Balsamic vinegar is made in and around Modena in Italy. Its rich, mellow flavor is perfect for Mediterranean-style salads, but if it is unavailable, use sherry vinegar or white wine vinegar instead.

Desserts

Don't forget the dessert—it can be cooked on the barbecue, too. Although desserts are not the most important part of a barbecue spread, they are always fun to cook and most can be prepared in advance and left above the cooling coals to cook to perfection while you dig into the main course.

Fruit is always a good choice because it contrasts so well with the often rich and filling main courses. Try croissants filled with chocolate and raspberries or panettone topped with marscapone cheese.

Have plenty of ice cream as a stand-by. It's popular with the children and is delicious served with barbecued fruits on a hot summer day. Thick, unsweetened yogurt or light cream are also ideal accompaniments. If you don't want a hot dessert, prepare a simple fruit salad.

For a quick sweet treat thread marshmallows onto skewers and hold them above the warm coals until just softened.

Barbecued Baked Apples

When they are wrapped in kitchen foil, apples bake to perfection on the barbecue and make a delightful finale to any meal.

Serves 4

INGREDIENTS

4 medium cooking apples
$1/4$ cup chopped walnuts
$1/4$ cup ground almonds
2 tablespoons light muscovado sugar

$1/4$ cup chopped cherries
2 tbsp preserved ginger, chopped
1 tbsp amaretto (almond-flavored liqueur) (optional)

4 tbsp butter
heavy cream or unsweetened yogurt, to serve

1 Core the apples and using a knife, score each one around the middle to prevent the apple skins from splitting during cooking.

2 To make the filling, mix together the walnuts, almonds, sugar, cherries, ginger, and amaretto, if using, in a small bowl.

3 Spoon the filling mixture into each apple, pushing it down into the hollowed-out core. Mound a little of the filling mixture on top of each apple.

4 Place each apple on a large square of double-thickness foil and generously dot all over with the butter. Wrap up the foil so that the apple is completely enclosed.

5 Cook the foil packets containing the apples over hot coals for 25–30 minutes, or until tender.

6 Transfer the apples to warm, individual serving plates. Serve with plenty of whipped heavy cream or thick unsweetened yogurt.

COOK'S TIP

If the coals are dying down, place the foil packets directly onto the coals, raking them up around the apples. Cook for 25–30 minutes and serve with the cream or yogurt.

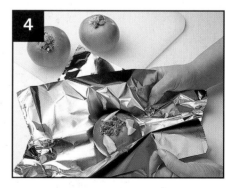

Fruity Skewers with Chocolate Dipping Sauce

These warm, lightly barbecued fruit kabobs
are served with a delicious chocolate dipping sauce.

Serves 4

INGREDIENTS

selection of fruit (choose from
  oranges, bananas, strawberries,
  pineapple chunks (fresh or canned),
  apricots (fresh or canned), eating
  apples, pears, kiwi fruit)
1 tbsp lemon juice

CHOCOLATE SAUCE:
4 tbsp butter
4 squares dark chocolate, broken into
  small cubes
$^1/_2$ tbsp cocoa powder
2 tbsp corn syrup

BASTE:
4 tbsp clear honey
grated rind and juice of $^1/_2$ orange

1 To make the chocolate sauce, place the butter, chocolate, cocoa powder, and corn syrup in a small pan. Heat gently at the side of the barbecue, stirring continuously, until all of the ingredients have melted and are well combined.

2 To prepare the fruit, peel and core if necessary, then cut into large, bite-size pieces or wedges as appropriate. Dip apples, pears, and bananas in lemon juice to prevent discoloration. Thread the pieces of fruit onto skewers.

3 To make the baste, mix together the honey, orange juice and rind, heat gently if required, and brush over the fruit.

4 Broil the fruit skewers over warm coals for 5–10 minutes, until hot. Serve with the chocolate dipping sauce.

COOK'S TIP

If the coals are too hot, raise the rack so that it is about 6 inches above the coals or spread out the coals a little to reduce the heat. Do not assemble the fruit skewers more than 1–2 hours before they are required.

Toffee Fruit Kabobs

Serve these fruit kabobs with a sticky toffee sauce. They are perfect for fall barbecues.

Serves 4

INGREDIENTS

2 eating apples, cored and cut
   into wedges
2 firm pears, cored and cut
   into wedges

juice of $^1/_2$ lemon
2 tbsp light muscovado sugar
$^1/_4$ tsp ground allspice
2 tbsp unsalted butter, melted

SAUCE:
9 tbsp butter
$^1/_2$ cup light muscovado sugar
6 tbsp heavy cream

1 Toss the apple and pears in the lemon juice to prevent any discoloration.

2 Mix the sugar and allspice together and sprinkle over the fruit.

3 Carefully thread the fruit pieces onto skewers.

4 To make the toffee sauce, place the butter and sugar in a saucepan and heat, stirring gently, until the butter has melted and the sugar has dissolved.

5 Add the cream to the saucepan and bring to a boil. Boil for 1–2 minutes, then set aside to cool slightly.

6 Meanwhile, place the fruit kabobs over hot coals and broil for about 5 minutes, turning and basting frequently with the melted butter, until the fruit is just tender.

7 Transfer the fruit kabobs to warm serving plates and serve with the slightly cooled toffee sauce.

COOK'S TIP

Firm apples that will keep their shape are needed for this dish—varieties such as Golden Delicious, Granny Smith and Braeburn are a good choice. Soft apples and pears will become mushy as they cook.

VARIATION

Sprinkle the fruit kabobs with chopped walnuts or pecans before serving, if you wish.

Chocolate & Raspberry Croissants

Simple to prepare, these tasty croissants are placed on the barbecue to warm through until the chocolate melts.

Serves

INGREDIENTS

4 butter croissants

4 tsp raspberry preserve

6 squares dark chocolate

3/4 cup raspberries

oil, for greasing

1 Slice the croissants in half. Spread the bottom half of each croissant with 1 teaspoon of the raspberry preserve.

2 Grate or finely chop the chocolate and sprinkle over the raspberry preserve.

3 Lightly grease 4 sheets of foil, brushing with a little oil.

4 Divide the raspberries equally among the croissants and replace the top half of each croissant. Place each croissant onto a sheet of foil, wrapping the foil around the croissant to enclose it completely.

5 Place the rack 6 inches above hot coals. Transfer the croissants to the rack and leave them to heat through for 10–15 minutes, or until the chocolate just begins to melt.

6 Remove the foil and transfer the croissants to individual serving plates. Serve hot.

VARIATION

For a delicious chocolate and strawberry filling for the croissants, use sliced strawberries and strawberry preserve instead of the raspberries.

VARIATION

You could also use milk chocolate or a mixture of milk and dark chocolate for this dish.

COOK'S TIP

Use the best quality fruit preserve you can find. Better still, use homemade jellies and preserves.

Baked Bananas

The orange-flavored cream can be prepared in advance but do not make up the banana packets until just before you need to cook them—they take only a few moments to get ready.

Serves 4

INGREDIENTS

4 bananas
2 passion fruit
4 tbsp orange juice
4 tbsp orange-flavored liqueur

ORANGE-FLAVORED CREAM:
$^2/_3$ cup heavy cream
3 tbsp confectioners' sugar

2 tbsp orange-flavored liqueur

1 Peel the bananas and place each one onto a sheet of foil.

2 Cut the passion fruit in half and squeeze the juice of each half over each banana. Spoon the orange juice and liqueur over each banana.

3 Fold the kitchen foil over the top of the bananas to enclose them completely.

4 Cook the bananas over hot coals for about 10 minutes, or until they are warm and just tender.

5 To make the orange-flavored cream, pour the heavy cream into a mixing bowl and sprinkle with the confectioners' sugar. Whisk the mixture until it is standing in soft peaks. Carefully fold in the orange-flavored liqueur and chill in the refrigerator until required.

6 Transfer the foil packets containing the bananas to warm, individual serving plates. Open the foil packets at the table and then serve the bananas immediately with the orange-flavored cream.

VARIATION

Leave the bananas in their skins for a really quick dessert. Split the banana skins and put in 1–2 squares of chocolate. Wrap the bananas in foil and barbecue for 10 minutes, or until the chocolate just melts.

Panettone with Mascarpone & Strawberries

Panettone is a sweet Italian bread. It is delicious toasted, and when it is topped with marscapone cheese and marinated strawberries it makes a sumptuous dessert.

Serves 4

INGREDIENTS

2 cups strawberries

$^1/_4$ cup superfine sugar

6 tbsp Marsala wine

$^1/_2$ tsp ground cinnamon

4 slices panettone

4 tbsp mascarpone cheese

1 Hull and slice the strawberries and place them in a bowl. Add the sugar, Marsala, and cinnamon to the strawberries.

2 Toss the strawberries in the sugar and cinnamon mixture until they are well coated. Chill in the refrigerator for at least 30 minutes.

3 When ready to serve, transfer the slices of panettone to a rack set over medium hot coals. Broil the panettone for about 1 minute on each side, or until golden brown.

4 Remove the panettone from the barbecue and transfer to serving plates. Top the panettone with the mascarpone cheese and the marinated strawberries. Serve immediately.

COOK'S TIP

Mascarpone is an Italian soft cheese with a rich, creamy texture, tasting like very thick cream. It will melt into the panettone, making it quite delicious. If mascarpone is unavailable, cream cheese or ricotta would be good alternatives.

VARIATION

Spread mascarpone cheese onto sweet biscuits that have been toasted on the barbecue.

Piña Colada Pineapple

The flavors of pineapple and coconut blend well together, as they do in the well-known drink Piña Colada. Here, barbecued pineapple is served with coconut for an equally special effect.

Serves 4

INGREDIENTS

1 small pineapple
4 tbsp unsalted butter

2 tbsp light muscovado sugar
$^2/_3$ cup grated fresh coconut,

2 tbsp coconut-flavored liqueur
or rum

1 Using a very sharp knife, cut the pineapple into quarters and then remove the tough core from the center, leaving the leaves attached.

2 Carefully cut the pineapple flesh away from the skin. Make horizontal cuts across the flesh of the pineapple quarters.

3 Place the butter in a pan and heat gently until melted, stirring continuously. Brush the melted butter over the pineapple and sprinkle with the sugar.

4 Cover the pineapple leaves with kitchen foil in order to prevent them from burning, and transfer them to a rack set over hot coals.

5 Broil the pineapple for about 10 minutes.

6 Sprinkle the coconut over the pineapple and broil, cut side up, for a further 5–10 minutes, or until the pineapple is piping hot.

7 Transfer the pineapple to serving plates and remove the foil from the leaves. Spoon a little coconut-flavored liqueur or rum over the pineapple and serve at once.

COOK'S TIP

Fresh coconut has the best flavor for this dish. If it is unavailable or you prefer, however, you can use shredded coconut.

Stuffed Pears with Mincemeat

*Pears quickly go soft and lose their shape when they are cooked,
so choose fruit with good firm flesh for this recipe.*

Serves 4

INGREDIENTS

4 firm pears
1 tsp lemon juice
2 tbsp mincemeat

5 tbsp cake crumbs or 4 amaretti
cookies, crushed

1 tbsp butter
ice cream, to serve

1 Using a sharp knife, cut the pears in half. Using a teaspoon, scoop out the core and discard.

2 Brush the cut surface of each of the pear halves with a little lemon juice to prevent discoloration.

3 Mix together the mincemeat and cake crumbs, or crushed amaretti cookies.

4 Divide the mixture among the pear halves, spooning it into a mound where the core has been removed.

5 Place 2 pear halves on a large square of double-thickness foil and generously dot all over with the butter.

6 Wrap up the foil around the pears so that they are completely enclosed.

7 Transfer the foil packets to a rack set over hot coals. Cook for 25–30 minutes, or until the pears are hot and just tender.

8 Transfer the pears to individual serving plates. Serve with 2 scoops of ice cream per serving.

VARIATION

Use mincemeat to stuff apples instead of pears, and bake them on the barbecue in the same way.

COOK'S TIP

If the coals are dying down, place the foil packets directly onto the coals and barbecue for 25–30 minutes.

Peaches with Creamy Mascarpone Filling

If you prepare these in advance, all you have to do is put the peaches on the barbecue when you are ready to serve them.

Serves 4

INGREDIENTS

4 peaches
1 cup mascarpone cheese

$^{1}/_{2}$ cup pecan or walnuts, chopped

1 tsp sunflower oil
4 tbsp maple syrup

1 Cut the peaches in half and remove the pits. If you are preparing this recipe in advance, press the peach halves together again and wrap them in plastic wrap until required.

2 Mix the mascarpone and pecan or walnuts together in a small bowl until well combined. Chill in the refrigerator until required.

3 To serve, brush the peaches with a little oil and place on a rack set over medium hot coals. Broil the peach halves for 5–10 minutes, turning once, until they are hot.

4 Transfer the peach halves to a serving dish and top with the mascarpone and nut mixture.

5 Drizzle the maple syrup over the peaches and mascarpone filling, and serve at once.

VARIATION

You can use nectarines instead of peaches for this recipe, if you prefer. Remember to choose ripe, but fairly firm, fruit which won't go soft and mushy when it is barbecued. Prepare the nectarines in the same way as the peaches and barbecue for 5–10 minutes.

COOK'S TIP

Mascarpone cheese is high in fat, so if you are following a low-fat diet, use thick unsweetened yogurt.

Exotic Fruity Packets

Delicious pieces of exotic fruit are warmed through in a deliciously scented, pomegranate-flavored sauce to make a fabulous barbecue dessert.

Serves 4

INGREDIENTS

1 papaya	1 tbsp grenadine	light cream or unsweetened yogurt,
1 mango	3 tbsp orange juice	to serve
1 star fruit		

1 Cut the papaya in half, scoop out the seeds with a spoon, and then discard the seeds. Peel the papaya and cut the flesh into thick slices.

2 Prepare the mango by cutting it lengthwise in half either side of the central pit.

3 Score each mango half in a criss-cross pattern. Push each mango half inside out to separate the cubes and cut them away from the peel.

4 Using a sharp knife, thickly slice the star fruit.

5 Place all of the fruit in a bowl and mix them together.

6 Mix the grenadine and orange juice together and pour over the fruit. Marinate for at least 30 minutes.

7 Divide the fruit among 4 double-thickness squares of foil and gather up the edges to form a packet that encloses the fruit.

8 Place the foil packet on a rack set over warm coals and barbecue the fruit for 15–20 minutes.

9 Serve the fruit in the packet, with light cream or yogurt on the side.

COOK'S TIP

Grenadine is a sweet syrup made from pomegranates. If you prefer, you could use pomegranate juice instead of the grenadine for this recipe. To extract the juice, cut the pomegranate in half and squeeze gently with a lemon squeezer—do not press too hard or the juice may become bitter.

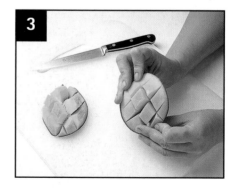

Index

Apples, barbecued baked 236
artichoke & prosciutto salad 222
avocado salsa 102

Bacon & scallop skewers 40
bananas, baked 244
bean curd skewers,
   marinated 174
beans:
   mixed bean salad 230
   vegetarian sausages 182
beef:
   barbecue steaks with red
      onion marmalade 104
   beef teriyaki 98
   beef tomato & olive
      kabobs 108
   beef toppers 96
   boozy beef steaks 100
   meatball brochettes 112
   Mexican steaks with avocado
      salsa 102
   steak & kidney kabobs 166
   surf & turf kabobs 106
   with mushrooms 110
bell pepper salad,
   Mediterranean 232
blackened fish 10
bread, garlic 202
bream, charbroiled 18
bruschetta, Mediterranean 204

Cabbage: coleslaw 208
Caesar salad 206
Cajun spicy chicken 60
Caribbean pork 144
Caribbean shrimp 44
cheese:
   eggplant &
      mozzarella sandwiches 186
   Italian mozzarella salad 220
chicken:
   Cajun spicy chicken 60
   chicken satay 68
   chicken skewers with lemon
      & cilantro 66
   chicken skewers with red
      bell pepper sauce 74
   chicken tikka 56
   favorite barbecued
      chicken 52
   Indian charred chicken 58
   jerk chicken 50
   Maryland chicken kabobs 76
   sesame chicken brochettes
      with cranberry sauce 72
   spatchcock baby chicken with
      garlic & herbs 62
   sticky drumsticks 54
   sweet maple chicken 64
   Thai-style chicken skewers 70
chocolate & raspberry
   croissants 242

cod, Indonesian-style spicy 8
coleslaw 208
corn cobs 198
cracked wheat: tabouleh 216
croissants, chocolate
   & raspberry 242

Desserts 235-54
duck:
   barbecued duckling 90
   citrus duckling skewers 86
   glazed duckling with
      pineapple salsa 92
   sesame orange duckling 88

Eggplant:
   eggplant & mozzarella
      sandwiches 186
   charbroiled eggplant 188

Fish & seafood 7-46
fruit:
   exotic fruity packets 254
   fruity skewers with chocolate
      dipping sauce 238
   toffee fruit kabobs 240

Garlic bread 202
green bean & carrot salad 210

Ham:
   ham & pineapple kabobs 156
   steaks with spicy apple
      rings 146
herrings:
   barbecued with lemon 36
   with orange tarragon
      stuffing 42

Indian charred chicken 58
Indian kofta 138
Indonesian-style spicy cod 8
Italian mozzarella salad 220

Japanese-style charbroiled
   flounder 24
jerk chicken 50

Kibbeh 122

Lamb:
   barbecued ribs 124
   burgers with mint & pine
      nuts 116
   butterfly chops with
      redcurrant glaze 118
   butterfly lamb with balsamic
      vinegar & mint 126
   cutlets with rosemary 134
   Indian kofta 138
   kibbeh 122
   Moroccan kabobs 130
   noisettes with tomato

salsa 142
   red wine lamb skewers 128
   shish kabobs 132
   sweet lamb fillet 140
   with a spice crust 120
   with mango & chili 136
lentil salad with balsamic
   dressing 218
liver:
   liver & onion kabobs 170
   sherried chicken liver
      brochettes 84

Mackerel:
   apricot charbroiled
      mackerel 28
   with lime & cilantro 30
mango & wild rice salad 228
Maryland chicken
   kabobs 76
meat 95-170
meatball brochettes 112
Mediterranean bell pepper salad
   232
Mediterranean bruschetta 204
Mediterranean-style
   sardines 32
Mexican steaks with avocado
   salsa 102
mixed broil skewers 168
monkfish:
   skewers with coconut &
      cilantro 14
   skewers with zucchini
      & lemon 12
Moroccan lamb kabobs 130
mushrooms, stuffed 196

Panettone with mascarpone &
   strawberries 246
pasta salad with basil
   vinaigrette 226
peaches with creamy
   mascarpone filling 252
pears: pear & Roquefort
   salad 224
   stuffed with mincemeat 250
pineapple:
   flounder, Japanese-style
      charbroiled 24
   Piña Colada 248
pork:
   Caribbean pork 144
   fruity pork skewers 152
   honey-glazed chops 158
   pork & apple skewers with
      mustard 148
   pork & sage kabobs 164
   ribs with plum sauce 150
   spicy pork ribs 154
   tangy pork tenderloin 162
potatoes:
   barbecued garlic

potato wedges 180
   crispy potato skins 176
   potato salad 214
poultry 47-92
pumpkin packets with chili
   & lime 200

Rice burgers, nutty 184

Salads 206-32
salmon:
   salmon brochettes 22
   salmon yakitori 20
sardines:
   Mediterranean-style 32
   with olives & tomatoes 38
sausages:
   vegetarian 182
   with barbecue sauce 160
scallops:
   bacon & scallop skewers 40
sea bream, charbroiled 18
seafood & fish 7-46
shish kabobs 132
shrimp:
   Caribbean shrimp 44
   herb & garlic shrimp 46
smoked cod:
   smoky fish skewers 26
spinach & orange salad 212
steak & kidney kabobs 166
surf & turf kabobs 106
sweet potato slices, spicy 178

Tabouleh 216
Thai-style chicken skewers 70
toffee fruit kabobs 240
tomatoes, stuffed 190
trout, nutty stuffed 34
tuna steaks, charred 16
turkey:
   charbroiled turkey with
      cheesy pockets 80
   spicy turkey & sausage
      kabobs 82
   turkey steaks with redcurrant
      glaze 78

Vegetables 173-200
   charbroiled mixed
      vegetables 194
   colorful vegetable
      kabobs 192
vegetarian sausages 182
venison steaks, charbroiled 114

Index compiled by Hilary Bird.